"Shannan Martin is a sidewalk poet and an everyday prophet. In *Start with Hello* she issues a stunning and accessible invitation for us to live as neighbors in the world, casting a hopeful vision of what it looks like to be human together. As it turns out, there is no *them* but only *us*, and this is the book we both want and need to help us find our way back to each other."

Emily P. Freeman, *Wall Street Journal* bestselling author of *The Next Right Thing*

"This book is so inspiring, but in a chill, regular sort of way. It doesn't wreck you or kick you in the pants or make you rethink your entire existence. Instead, it will change you by helping you see the beauty of where you currently exist and the people who exist near you. It makes being a neighbor, not to mention a person, just so beautifully . . . *doable*. Y'all, this is the book we've been waiting for."

Kendra Adachi, *New York Times* bestselling author of *The Lazy Genius Way*

"Fellow wallflowers, Shannan Martin has written our guide to come to the dance floor in a way that feels possible, alluring, and bursting with potential. In terms that are both poetic and practical, Shannan makes a compelling case that we all can find our people and our places in community. *Start with Hello* invites us to see the people around us as whole and generous and just waiting to be known and loved. You'll want to mark up your copy and pass it to a neighbor."

Beth Silvers, cohost of the *Pantsuit Politics* podcast and coauthor of *Now What?*

"'Jen, pick one of your favorite people on planet Earth.' Fine, I pick Shannan. I pick her friendship. I pick her example. I pick *Start with Hello*. This book. It is lovely, warm, honest. It brims with possibility. It is—and Shannan would hate this word—inspiring. I want to run home and leave the mess where it is and send a text to my five closest neighbors to come over for chili and $10 wine. What a gift she is. What a gif

Jen H author, host of *For t* y Collective

"In her wise, loving, practical, and timely book, Shannan Martin dispels all that is mystical about being a good neighbor. *Start with Hello*. It's just that simple but we can overthink it, and this is where I'm so grateful we have Shannan to lead us. We do this, Shannan reminds us, by first being curious and aware of those around us. Filled with her disarming sense of humor, *Start with Hello* is a love letter to community and a call to action toward radical, realistic hospitality."

Osheta Moore, pastor, speaker, and author of *Dear White Peacemakers*

"*Start with Hello* is winsome, kind, and brave—exactly what we need in times like these. I'm grateful for the ways Shannan not only helps us lean into growth but also shows us how to compassionately embody it."

Aundi Kolber, therapist and author of *Try Softer* and *The Try Softer Guided Journey*

"*Start with Hello* is an impactful read. Shannan does not hold back in addressing anti-racism. She highlights the importance of loving your neighbor and treating people with dignity and respect, while also providing practical tools to help assist you in understanding those you perceive to be different from you."

Faitth Brooks, writer, speaker, and educator

"I forever want Shannan Martin to boss me on the art of neighboring and the true purpose of home. One of the best books of the year."

Myquillyn Smith, *New York Times* bestselling author of *Welcome Home*

"See, this is why I love Shannan Martin! In *Start with Hello*, she gives the reader amazingly practical steps that help us move toward one another in an age where we seem to be moving further apart. She reminds us that although our daily activities may not change the whole world, if we are each intentional about these ten subtle shifts, we could most definitely change our individual worlds."

Jonathan "Pastah J" Brooks, author of *Church Forsaken*

"This essential field guide to expanding your world (in spite of all that makes us human) is engaging, accessible, and beautifully layered with Shannan's signature storytelling and unabashed honesty. You'll be better for reading it, and so will the world around you."

Deidra Riggs, author of *30 Days to Being Actively Anti-Racist on Social Media*

"*Start with Hello* has changed the way I see my neighborhood, challenged the way I define and live in community, and given me hope that we can actually build a better world for us to live in by taking small steps to connect with one another. Read it, practice the simple ways you can move toward each other, and begin to experience the richness of heaven here on earth."

Grace P. Cho, writer, poet, and editor

"*Start with Hello* is a required read for anyone who cares about community—a roadmap back into authentic communities. Martin delivers an easy read with delightful wit as she leans into uncomfortable truths about building connections. Her experiences are relatable and give us needed wisdom to develop meaningful relationships with estranged neighbors in today's America."

José Chiquito Galván, writer and Shannan's actual neighbor

"Shannan Martin takes us by the hand and leads us on a journey of true human connection in her new book, *Start with Hello*. This beautiful and practical reflection beckons us to come as we are so that we may experience the depths of our humanity. Borrowing Shannan's own words, it is 'an invitation to belong more fully and engage more deeply with this life we've been given.' With thoughtfulness and vulnerability, this book shows us what it really means to be a neighbor and a friend."

Kat Armas, author of *Abuelita Faith* and host of *The Protagonistas* podcast

Books by Shannan Martin

Falling Free
The Ministry of Ordinary Places
Start with Hello

START WITH HELLO

(And Other Simple Ways to Live as Neighbors)

SHANNAN MARTIN

Revell

a division of Baker Publishing Group
Grand Rapids, Michigan

Published by Revell
a division of Baker Publishing Group
PO Box 6287, Grand Rapids, MI 49516-6287
www.revellbooks.com

Printed in the United States of America

Library of Congress Cataloging-in-Publication Data
Names: Martin, Shannan, 1976– author.
Title: Start with hello : (and other simple ways to live as neighbors) / Shannan Martin.
Description: Grand Rapids, MI : Revell, a division of Baker Publishing Group, [2022] | Includes bibliographical references.
Identifiers: LCCN 2022001823 | ISBN 9780800742379 (casebound) | ISBN 9780800740894 (paperback) | ISBN 9781493438945 (ebook)
Subjects: LCSH: Friendship—Religious aspects—Christianity.
Classification: LCC BV4647.F7 M373 2022 | DDC 241/.6762–dc23/eng/20220214
LC record available at https://lccn.loc.gov/2022001823

Published in association with Yates & Yates, www.yates2.com

Baker Publishing Group publications use paper produced from sustainable forestry practices and post-consumer waste whenever possible.

22 23 24 25 26 27 28   7 6 5 4 3 2 1

For Cal, Ruby, Silas, and Robert.
My favorite first hellos.

When it is all too much . . . and a single life feels too small a stone to offer on the altar of Peace, find a Human Sunrise. Find those people who are committed to changing our scary reality. Human sunrises are happening all over the earth, at every moment.

Alice Walker

Contents

CHAPTER 1

Awake > Asleep

> We stay awake, believing attentiveness is our
> road map to meaningful community.

I AM SEVENTEEN YEARS OLD IN A TINY, working-class town in Ohio. It's a school night, but my friends and I can drive so we do, tracing back roads like our five-year-old hands on construction paper in Miss Beam's kindergarten class. We've been together for thirteen years, fated by birth dates and a zip code, connected by shared experiences and the place we call home. Parents split, innumerable basketball games won and lost, physics tests crammed for and (mostly) passed, snow days and trampolines and square pizza in the same cramped cafeteria. One more month and we'll disperse. One of my friends turns up the radio as Tim McGraw croons and I say, again, that I have no respect for country music. But this time loss sinks in my chest like a rock tossed into a river. My body knows what my heart can't comprehend. This sort of easy, uncomplicated belonging is a memory I'll spend decades chasing. My eyes well up in the dark as I sit squeezed in the back seat of someone's dad's Dodge. Everything is about to change. (This is the night I secretly start to like country music.)

I AM TWENTY-THREE, living in a basement apartment in a complex nicknamed "Stabbin' Cabins" because of the disproportionate incidence of, well, homicide. I'm barely married. My husband, Cory, spends his weekdays living out of town, finishing a college internship. I work sixty hours a week at a car rental company, washing SUVs while wearing a business suit, and spend my free time wondering how I let it happen. My parents are three hours away but it might as well be thirty. I'm adrift, a misfit. It turns out marriage, even on its best days, can't erase my longing for a wider web of attachment. I'm an adult but also a child. I still like country music because I'm still sort of sad.

I AM TWENTY-FIVE in Washington, DC, taking the Red Line home from work and picking up the pieces of a marriage spun sideways. We live near the sort of wealth and power that smell like Italian shoe leather and the butane flame of catered lunches. Here, adults seem somehow *more* adult, happy and at ease, as if they really do hold the keys to their futures. I feel glaringly out of place. Shockingly Midwestern. There's a Pottery Barn (the height of sophistication) and a Chipotle (I mispronounce it for the duration) across the street, but *my* shoes are from TJ Maxx, and Cory and I have just one friend between us.

I AM THIRTY, the mom of two babies born in one year, in love with my unexpected family. I try wrangling purpose from our broken-record days by way of sleep schedules and library books. I'm grounded and unmoored, never alone and always lonely. I start a blog one night and find solidarity on the internet. My world cracks open like a geode, new friendships across time zones shimmering in my hands. Who knew my laptop screen could be a portal to belonging? Real-life connection remains mostly out of reach. My closest neighbors are soybeans and corn. Life on a farm is what I thought I wanted, but long lanes don't lend themselves easily to the clash with ordinary people I crave.

I AM THIRTY-FIVE, brand-new to the neighborhood, a shy introvert yet desperate to be known. I catch a glimpse of what life could look like if we all took one step closer to each other, unbothered by our differences. Slowly, I stop wishing to receive an invitation to belong and start writing my own. Unsure of where to begin, I set out to be the neighbor I long for.[i] This begins a decade of catch and release, where I take turns reaching out to the people close to me and they do the same. On paper most of us have little in common. But

---

i. I use the term *neighbor* with every ounce of flexibility it affords. These are the people whose homes surround my own but also anyone whose path crosses mine, at any given moment and in any manifestation. What I'm trying to say is, Hi, neighbor!

on sidewalks and along alleys we discover we want the same things: to trust and be trusted, to be seen and believed, to be generous. We want the security that comes with knowing we aren't alone in this disorienting world.

I AM FORTY-FIVE with miles to go, but I have learned some things along the way. I've learned to depend on a hot cup of black tea every single morning. I've learned there's more than one way to build a family. I've learned to heed my tears and take advice from peonies. I've learned to value listening and learning and to allow space for growth in the hearts of everyone, myself included. I've learned almost everything is some shade of beautiful if viewed from the right angle.

I have learned we're all aching for connection.

To *be* connected.

It's not just us. It's not just here. There is no zip code, no cul-de-sac, no apartment complex, subdivision, or stretch of dirt road that isn't pulsing with possibility. The question is, How do we do it? Where do we start?

How, Indeed?

It's not unrealistic to want the easier connection of childhood in the thick of adulthood. It's not asking too much. It's remembering what we've forgotten. It's recognizing, again, how we were built and what we were made for. It's waking up to a dauntless, kid-size vision for friendship and holding hope that it's out here, waiting for us.

It's attainable. And worth fighting for.

We have pastors and priests and spiritual advisors to guide our faith. We have doctors and therapists to care for our bodies and minds. We have teachers to show us how to write sonnets, form hypotheses, and drive a car. But no one teaches us that community has to be built with our hands and our tender hearts and our precious time. No one breaks it all the way down. No one gives us the tools. From the outside looking in, it can seem like community just happens for the lucky few. It's easy to assume we're the ones getting it wrong.

I'm not here to tell anyone how to fix their life. That's not what this book is about. I never get enough sleep or exercise. I haven't figured out how to inspire my kids to do their chores without reminders or brush their teeth without being told. My husband and I still argue about who should be scrubbing the bathroom. And we recently took out a loan to buy a used minivan, even though we were taught to pay cash.

What I *can* tell you, with confidence, is that living in close connection with other humans has made my life brighter, weirder, and better. This is among the truest truths of my life. Learning to live with "neighbor" as part of my DNA has changed the way I see the world and myself. It has changed who I am and what I believe in.

In some ways this learning process has taken me back to my childhood roots, where I fully expected the quirks and disappointments of myself and the people around me.

In other ways it burned the book of loneliness, that age-old tale, and opened for me a basic spiral notebook—the freshest of fresh starts (just-sharpened pencil smells, free of charge).

I've also collected my fair share of mistakes. In hindsight, most were made when I retreated too far inward, overthinking things and trying too hard. I've lost my way when I forced connection out of a sense of obligation rather than surrendering to the simple fact that my well-being depends on the solace and safety a network of other humans provides.

We take what we learn and till it into the soil. Imperfections make for good fertilizer, but we have to root them out first. Unflinching honesty will be helpful along the way; so will humility and humor.

More than anything, we'll need a hearty dose of childlike imagination. Do we believe there's a better option than the one we've been given? Like, *really* believe it?

Baby Steps + Popsicle Sticks

If you're like me,[ii] you might be skeptical that life could be brighter with the added complication of other people and all their tangled messes. Maybe you're afraid I'm trying to trick you into doing things you're not ready to do. Or maybe you've read other books that talk a lot about table settings and charcuterie (pass the salami!) but don't quite fill in the gaps on how to get from *right here* (picture frumpy feelings, two-day sweatpants, an aversion to small talk) to the rest of it.

Let me be clear—this is not a hospitality book, though we will talk about what "home" means for us as regular,

---

ii. Naturally wary, a bit grizzled at the edges, slightly jaded. Take your pick.

frazzled people learning the value of togetherness amid jobs and toddlers and roommates who oppress us by never closing the cabinet doors.

This is also not a shame-on-you book. Shame builds walls, and when it comes to walls, we're good. (Sigh.) This is not a "me" book. It's an "us" book.

I'm laying out the simplest path between us with the promise that when we meet in the middle, we'll find ourselves breathing easier. Our struggle, if anything, will be to trust the process, though that sounds a bit clichéd and overearnest.

Let's try this. Remember the movie *What About Bob?* I managed to live well into my forties before my psyche was forever pierced by Bob's enduring-if-bizarre wisdom. My kids howled through it, and now Bob's "baby steps" remain a somewhat intrusive source of perspective when life feels daunting in the Martin house.

Baby steps to each other. That's what this is about.

We could also think of my son Silas, who came downstairs with his professional-grade hot glue gun and told me his class was finishing the school year with a "passion project." The project he envisioned was to build a replica of his beloved school out of popsicle sticks. (He'd already secured permission to bring his own tools.)

When it comes to his passion, every single popsicle stick serves a purpose. When it comes to ours, there will be no step or stick too insignificant to mention. We can't risk not getting granular enough.

How do we fix the vexing cultural diagnoses of isolation, division, and despair? By making (and sustaining) contact.

I've got one foot in a rip current. You're throwing me a life preserver. Everything hinges on whether the rope is long enough, whether we are strong enough, to make contact.

The strength we need is not the typical kind, thank God. I say this as a woman who has never been strong of body and has been too strong, at times, of will. Stubbornness has its place and muscles are great for moving things, but the brawn we need is of the heart and soul.

We need grit.

We need resilience.

If we're ever going to make it to each other, we need to swim in the current of empathy for a while. We need to learn to really *see* each other.

Because until we do, our attempts at meaningful connection—the kind that transcends all we've been taught (which honestly isn't much)—will not have the relational muscle to sustain us.

Until then, our efforts at hospitality will ring hollow. I'm reminded of the terrorist-turned-preacher who once wrote that, without love, our efforts are a "clanging cymbal."[iii] Which is another way of saying that without true connectedness, our cheese boards are just random lumber and fancy raisins.

Vision School

How, then, do we wake up to each other? I'm thrilled you asked.

iii. 1 Corinthians 13:1.

Remember our agreement that when it comes to building the future of us, there's no stick too small? Here's what I'm asking you to do.

Start paying closer attention to the sky. For me, this happened accidentally.

As poets, theologians, and anxious parents of teenagers have said, we become what we love. Our influences shape us and so do our habits. Prior to ten or so years ago, I didn't give the sky much thought. I went about my business each day without considering that the earth, my flesh-and-bone body, and the connected life I longed for were inextricably woven together.

There are plenty of ways to split a worldview open. For my family it meant selling our farmhouse and moving to an overlooked, underwhelming neighborhood tucked behind some railroad tracks. The first time I stared out at our new city lot with its lopsided, postage-stamp yard, I told Cory, without a shred of irony or charm, "I guess I'll have to adjust to a life without beauty."

(I can't type that sentence without cackling. I'm just here, reporting the facts.)

I lacked imagination back then. I didn't yet know that beauty lives everywhere, calling from the sky and the earth below for us to notice—to be curious, to let ourselves feel small, and to see how we all fit into a bigger picture.

I have so much compassion for the woman I was then, but *mercy*. How was I so confused about this stunning world, where not a single corner is untouched by the buzz of wonder?

Courtney E. Martin writes that our attention "is spent one small, seemingly mundane choice at a time." She continues, "Ensure that your tiny choices reflect your grand ambitions for how people experience you and how you experience the world. It's all you've really got."[1]

I didn't know how to see differently. I hadn't learned to love past the familiar.

Paying attention to the sky taught me to bear witness to the present moment and my particular place, regardless of what they might hold. Life carries on, but *this* moment will never exist again. Creating a rhythm of attentiveness awakens us to possibility and tunes our hearts to the key of wonder. The sky belongs to everyone—the longest-living art installation.

But what do clouds have to do with people, Shannan?

I don't entirely know. It's just that the more intently I watch the sky, the more I behold the unflinching beauty around me. Inescapable. Everywhere. Not a day passes that I'm not struck by the grace and soul of this living treasure hidden behind the tracks.

The ground is our teacher. The sky is our guide. We exist against a backdrop of uncompromising artistry. I know that sounds woo-woo, but it doesn't have to. In an interview with radio host Krista Tippett, Irish poet and self-described agnostic Michael Longley said it like this: "For me, celebrating the wildflowers or the birds is like a kind of worship."[2]

Why would we want to take these things for granted when instead we could open our eyes and simply accept their invitation to vision school?

Start with Hello

I was taught it's good to love my neighbors, yet for a long time I assumed not *hating* my neighbors was enough. I didn't really know them but I definitely didn't hate them. Cool?

This new craving to get to know the people near me initially came with a few hurdles.

- I am an introvert. Deeply. Wholly. I could survive for many days without human contact of any kind. (Please make me prove it!)
- I am emotionally allergic to small talk.
- In the vibrantly diverse place I call home, there exists a language barrier between myself and some of my neighbors that my 2.5 years of distracted high school Spanish cannot overcome.
- I'm awkward. Just, in general.

On the one hand, I was lonely.

On the other hand, was it really necessary to talk to anyone who lived outside my home, ever?

I wanted to know people and to be known. But I felt like I'd been preloaded with the wrong personality. Just the thought of it was overwhelming and nerve-racking.

I fell into a plan of sorts, based on zero research or best practices. Enticing, right?

It worked.

Here's what I (accidentally) did and now stand by as an Official Plan.

Take Walks

I started to walk my kids to school every day—rain, snow, or shine.

These walks were a commitment to spending unhurried time in my place. This new rhythm pulled me from the shadows of modern living, where cars are swallowed up by garages and we could, realistically, go weeks without physically being seen.

Practically speaking, walking to school was about a more peaceful start to the day for myself and my kids. The shift I felt when we quit driving[iv] was profound and immediate. For once I was prioritizing connection over efficiency, and the effects were clear. Even when one of us was off to a rocky start we were in it together, sometimes even holding hands. It was the tiniest of rituals but it stuck.

My trip back home had a different focus. I was heading back into the meat of my workday. There are no faster hours than from 8:00 to 3:00 for a work-from-home parent. But for ten minutes I was alone in the quiet. Not doing but just *being*.

My neighbors made the same round trip. I started to recognize where some of them lived. They grew familiar to me, without us ever sharing words. I imagine I became familiar to them too.

Fall turned to spring and we rounded the corner from basic familiarity to smiles and hellos.

Confession: along these slow, small steps, I began harboring

---

iv. I'm too ashamed to tell you how close we live to the school and how ridiculous it is that we drove even once. Fine, the school is 2.5 blocks away. Bless my heart.

fantasies. I imagined inviting a particular woman over for tea. I daydreamed about us taking walks together, her pushing her baby in a stroller. Maybe we would become best friends. Maybe it would all play out like a charming TV show. Maybe! Alas, none of those dreams materialized. Not a single one. Maybe I waited too long. Maybe (probably) I stepped back in fear, believing the timing was never perfect enough or being afraid I would put her on the spot. It's within the realm of reason that I missed opportune moments along the way.

It's also possible that *hello* and *good morning* were always exactly enough. We aren't meant to become BFFs with every single person we encounter.

But it was a comfort to begin to recognize some of the faces around me. I still see their homes every day—lemon yellow, beige, gray with blue trim—and wonder how they're doing. Maybe one day I'll learn more. For now, it feels good to look from east to west and have a solid awareness of my place.

My family is past the elementary-school years now but we still do our best to carry this practice with us as we drive across town to the middle and high schools. On one morning commute, Cal pointed out the Amtrak train blazing down the tracks. Ruby, the Martin least likely to offer commentary, mused aloud, "I'll bet the passengers are thinking 'Goshen looks like a pretty place.'"

Affection is infectious. In the words of philosopher Simone Weil, "Attention is the rarest and purest form of generosity."[3]

Whether we're walking kids to school, riding the same bus each morning, or braving the same crowded break room each evening, connection awaits in the dust and crumbs of our daily lives.

Revolutions are grown from the soil of common longing, but we'll never know what we don't see.

Look Alive!

The best news is that we actually have plenty of time.

Earlier today, over red curry and drunken noodles, my friend Holly told me about the neighbor she finally met. In the midst of the COVID-19 pandemic, when the chips were nothing but down, they were there for each other, offering help and basic human contact. "It only took us seventeen years!" Holly laughed.

Seventeen years.

That's the thing. There's no expiration date or deadline for forging authentic, enduring relationships. We are free to take it slowly. We live our lives trusting that the tiny moments will not be wasted.

There is no such thing as a trivial connection. You might never bake that peach coffee cake with the perfect crumb and serve it to *her* in your living room at 8:00 a.m. on a Thursday.

But it might happen that one day you'll meet your son's classmate's mom. A few weeks later you might notice her driving by as you walk home. You'll wave. She'll wave back.

One day she'll pull up to the curb and ask a question. Eventually she'll come inside and sit at your table, and you'll swap stories of struggle and success.

After another year has passed she'll invite you into her home. You'll sit at her table and wrap your hands around

THERE
IS NO SUCH
THING AS A
TRIVIAL
CONNECTION.

her mug. She'll spread your toast with butter and sprinkle it with cinnamon. You'll talk about sorrow and motherhood until the tea grows cold.

You will have made an actual friend, slowly, over time. (And you will tear up, retelling the story.)

None of this would have happened if you hadn't decided to be the sort of person who looks people in the eye and says hello.

The Order of Things

I'm ten years into trying (and failing and regrouping and struggling and sometimes actually winning) at living awake and available to the world I'm in. What I'm still learning is that there truly is no space between us. My place, this neighborhood, is my training camp for connection. What I learn filters out past the geography of the Chamberlain neighborhood in Goshen, Indiana. These lessons bleed into my city, into my deeper, local friendships, into my real and meaningful online relationships. Even into my family life.

I used to get this backward. I assumed I could spend my efforts where I was most comfortable, in my own home, with my closest friends, and maybe in trusted, comfortable spaces like church. I could grow as a human behind closed doors, then carry the lessons out into the world around me, a steadier, more compassionate citizen.

The problem is, this work requires practice. Discovering a path toward closeness means bumbling about and trying again on the other side of that closed door, steadier and more comfortable over time.

Additionally, it's easy to get sidetracked and stuck. The circus of home-life and work-life and everyday-adult-life will always take over, if we let it. In two weeks alone, my family juggled birthdays, baseball tryouts, an illness, a couple of migraine headaches, a larger-than-normal marital spat, an emergency run for tennis shoes the night before they were needed, and a tsunami of tears as is commonplace in a household with three teenagers. This doesn't take into account jobs, school, and the fact that everyone starts sniffing around for dinner each night at 6:00.

Without some real intention, it wouldn't cross my mind to carry my relational scraps out into the world. Immersed in familiarity and sameness, I wouldn't know what I was missing, the swirling seas of contrast and creativity. I would miss out on that inexplicable *ta-da!* feeling that lands when I meet someone who challenges my tired ideas, making me feel hyperalive.

If I allowed myself to operate from a "mine first" mentality—my family, my home, my preferred social cliques—I would collapse each evening in a heap of fleece and tortilla chip crumbs, certain my time and bandwidth were exhausted by the daily grind, nothing left over to give.[v]

I'm a big fan of the fleece-and-crumbs liturgy, and nothing will change that. But I have more capacity than I often

---

v. The real goal of this project is to begin to see connection as interwoven into our regular lives, which means it can—and should—exist even when we're at our fleeciest. But I'm getting ahead of myself! Just trust that I'll never try to wrangle you out of your easy britches, and I believe in the comfort and quiet of home at the end of a long day.

think I do. When we orient our identities around community, the "all in this together," we see there is enough for everyone. Enough time. Enough attention. Even for me. This doesn't mean abandoning the duties and loves of my life. It means being thoughtfully aware that a connected life offers abundantly more.

In those small, fleeting moments when a hello leads to some delicious pan dulce, I gain entry into a wider web of inclusion. I get out among people and learn to *see*. I collect more data on what it means to be fully alive in this particular chaos and in the precise brilliance that is *now*.

For many of us this is soul-stretching work. We might feel rusty after long stretches of quiet. For some of us the compounding divisions associated with just being alive have left scars. We're guarded. Skeptical. Cynical, even.

Just remember: baby steps. I'm not asking you to take a girls' trip with anyone or spill your guts to the next person you encounter. I'm just nudging you to admire the sky, take a walk, and say hello.

Here's the thing. If my sample size only includes me, Cory, the kids, and our dearest friends, my theories on life will be simple but skewed. When I widen my lens, bringing more into view, gathering and sorting and placing it all beneath the microscope of compassion and care, the results are more complicated.

That's where the magic is.

Those are the ambiguities and question marks and clap emojis I bring home with me—because no matter what, home is always waiting.

If I were a politician or an economist I might call this "trickle-down connection."

Alas, I am just one woman, a citizen of today, a friend, a wife, a mom. A neighbor. I've seen the way shared bonds make humans a little more whole. From the sky to the ground, from our bodies to our hearts, into our homes and back out to the streets, this is the circuitry of us.

We awaken and awaken and awaken ourselves because the world outside is not scary or separate. It's what holds us together.

We face it with arms linked and eyes wide because *we* are the electricity we don't want to miss.

A Glimpse of Possibility

It's a Saturday morning in the last dregs of August, cooler than normal, the sort of late summer day that signals a season's end.

I'm up at 6:00 a.m., unusual for me on a weekend, but there are cinnamon rolls to cut and bake for my family and our out-of-town guests.

I wash the flour from my hands and drape the pan with a towel, hoping the second rise comes quickly.

I settle into my favorite spot on the couch with my mug of Earl Grey and a book. The sun begins its ascent over Main Street, over the tops of the walnut trees behind our house, over us. *Wake up, wake up.*

I inhale the steam from my tea, waiting until the temperature is just right, glad for the quiet. The doorbell rings.

I pull my cardigan tighter. There on the other side of the screen door is one of our neighbors: Mack, sixteen and still sleepy. He half-whispers, "I'm sorry if I woke you up. I was just wondering if you guys are coming to my football game at ten? Your company can come too."

"We'll be there," I say, pressing my palm against the screen as he reaches up and holds his against it, an odd high-five.

This is the flow. Can you feel it?

These are the moments that make up our lives.

There's no relationship or friendship or bonus-parentship that doesn't start somewhere thimble-size. A hello. A shared laugh. A quick helping hand. Viewed through the lens of enduring friendship, these aren't throwaway pleasantries. They are seeds.

Mack was eleven when we first met. He was twelve when he first came inside our house, thirteen when he ran the summer streets with Cal and his brothers, fourteen on our back patio and restless as his mom and I chatted too long, fifteen when he missed the bus and I drove him to school. Sixteen when he hoped we would be there cheering in the stands.

It matters, to my family and to Mack's, to know that we are just up the street from one another. Our connectedness poses no inconvenience. Having each other's backs takes nothing from us. We see each other. We notice. We wake up ready to care.

This is what makes us more human.

ONE SIMPLE WAY
to Live as Neighbors

Here's my favorite "waking up" practice, which conveniently converges walking, sky-staring, and noticing the inherent beauty of my place.

Once a month I walk to the same little corner of my neighborhood and take a photo. Because I'm a woman of the times, I usually post it on Instagram with a hashtag I created, #shannans8thspotalley. People seem to enjoy following along but I honestly do it for myself. This small practice helps ground me to my place as I notice what changes and what stays the same.

It helps me to see more clearly, which helps me love more authentically.

Want to join me? Choose your own favorite corner and begin documenting it each month. After a handful of times you'll start to see subtle changes emerge as time and nature and life carry on. Take it another tiny step forward and jot some notes about what's going on in your life each time you take the picture. Things change and things stay the same. We change and we stay the same. But through it all we can stay awake to the wonder and possibility around us.

CHAPTER 2

Windows > Mirrors

> We pursue beauty in difference, not in reflections
> of ourselves.

IT WAS THE SECOND CONSECUTIVE Easter Sunday that
my family wasn't at church.

Our first absence was explained away by a global pandemic.

This time we made our choice, and it was a road trip
to a new-to-us Midwestern city. For two days we traipsed
uncharted territory, sinking our feet into someone else's
good earth, settling into their shoes, imagining a different
kind of life where every home was palatial and every yard
sign cheered for the same team.

Wherever we travel, when we wander through unfamiliar neighborhoods I imagine what it's like to live in them.
*Do these people walk through the door at the end of the day
and feel the same comfort I do? Do they cozy up sometimes,*

wearing PJs and boiling spaghetti and reading on the couch? Do they have company over? Do they feel like they belong? This trip was no different. I drank my morning tea by leaded-glass windows and wondered how it would feel to be transplanted here, where people with graying temples have cocktails on their porches at dusk and every child on a bike wears a helmet.

In many ways it reminded me of the life we left behind when we moved to our current neighborhood—peaceful and gleaming. A rare pang of longing landed in my chest. Later, on a walk to the Lake Michigan shore, we took turns choosing our favorite house on each block. "Do you think any of these people know their neighbors?" I asked out loud. The kids groaned, weary of my one-track mind.

For those two days the most honest part of me remembered the allure of living in a world so earnestly manicured and conventionally beautiful. Wouldn't it be a relief not to have competing flags flanking the street, flying *at* each other? Wouldn't it be a comfort to exist apart from the sort of lack that peels the roof back in patches and rains on what's left exposed? To live sheltered from chained dogs and porches that wear the trauma of their inhabitants? To not constantly feel a spotlight shining on my own abundance?

The God's-honest truth is that I know these are lovely people. Their lives might be different from mine but aren't necessarily better—and probably aren't worse. Their bodies fail them. Their drains clog. Dinner burns so hard not even the skillet can be salvaged. They cry at night. They lose their way.

Just like me. Just like us.

My family was drawn to the vibrance of our neighborhood. Back then it almost seemed a bit romantic, this notion of diversity and difference. We'd lived so long without it. Ten years later and reality has long settled over us. Our place is vibrant and bleak. It's noisy and peaceful. It's uncomfortable. It's home.

Beautiful lives can be tremendously sad.

And sad-looking places can be tremendously beautiful.

Where we live shapes our worldview, for better or for worse. No matter our zip code, it's up to us to search for contrast even while we love the ground where we're planted.

Class Is in Session

There's something to be said for the comfort of similarity. We're biologically hardwired to seek the familiar; we often gravitate toward it without even meaning to. Biologists and anthropologists credit this genetic bent toward what's known with keeping the human species alive. We learn to trust those near us, those who tend to be "like" us, on primal levels. Watching them for cues, we are conditioned to avoid unfamiliar scenarios that signal danger at the cellular level.

The problem is, our bodies were never telling us to fear other *people*.

And yet the feedback loop tightens. *We're alive! We're safe!* The people near us, people we see as *like* us, keep us protected and calm. Slowly, imperceptibly, we inch away from those who do not, on a base level, remind us of ourselves.

This cultural and/or biological conditioning does us no favors and causes actual harm. It forces us apart and fences us into invisible camps where we only see each other from a distance. Unreachable, we turn inward. We retreat. And while having like-minded friends with some shared cultural shorthand can be a gift, if that is our only source of connection we wind up feeling adrift.

That's how we got here.

The word *xenophobia* has come to mean the fear of people from other countries, though that definition belies its deeper meaning. Derived from the Greek word *xenos*, xenophobia actually means the fear of the stranger or foreigner. Boiled down to its essence it means the fear of "the other," which poses an immediate threat to a multicultural nation of people who live largely segregated lives.[i]

Throughout history our politicians, inextricably bound to a culture of war, have taught us to be wary of people from certain countries. Even so, most of us would say we are not wholesale-scared of a particular nation. Our actual habits and behaviors, on the other hand, suggest that we have not actively fought against a tribalistic mindset. Over time, our central nervous system has been conditioned to hit the panic button whenever we encounter "the other," anyone we don't immediately identify as one of us.

i. This concludes the Shannan Martin Truly Oversimplified Version™ of the history of xenophobia.

Examining Our Histories

We avoid speaking honestly about this. I get it. If there was ever a risky time to say out loud (or in print), "I harbor biases against people I see as different from me," this would be it. It's okay to examine the patterns of our lives and realize we'd like to try something new. We don't have to be afraid and we're not in trouble. Accepting hard truths about ourselves means we're open to rediscovery and improvement. Just look at us grow!

If we want to clear this relational debris and build a stronger future together, we're going to have to come clean about what holds us back. I'll go first.

The first three decades of my life occurred in spaces where everyone mirrored me. From my bus driver, teachers, coaches, and pastors to the kids I babysat, the mail carrier, and the cashier at our shoebox of a grocery store, my entire community consisted of White,[ii] Protestant, working-class people. We shared the same politics. We went to similar churches on Sundays. We existed on carby Midwestern casseroles and sweet corn grown in our backyard gardens.

This collective uniformity blinded me to the most basic understanding of *difference*. Sure, I knew not everyone in the world was just like me. But my nonexistent exposure to anyone who looked, lived, or believed differently ensured

---

ii. As it relates to racial identity, I will be capitalizing both Black and White throughout the book, and I acknowledge this is a complex question with no clear consensus. To better understand my choice, see Ann Thúy Nguyễn and Maya Pendleton, "Recognizing Race in Language: Why We Capitalize 'Black' and 'White'," Center for the Study of Social Policy, March 23, 2020, https://cssp.org/2020/03/recognizing-race-in-language-why-we-capitalize-black-and-white/.

I never faced the tension of contrasting perspectives. My worldview remained safely unchecked, to the point I'm not even sure I thought of it as a worldview.

It was just "the way things were." The air I breathed. And I was poorer for it. It is our refusal to thoroughly examine these contours of life that allows evils like prejudice and racism to quietly bake into our bones. It is up to us to carefully pick through our histories and our present realities in order to uproot anything standing in the way of our wide embrace of one another.

Fast-forward to 2011.

When my family moved from an insular community to the neighborhood, we found instant proximity with people carrying a broad range of cultures, beliefs, and life experiences. The tension surrounding our move was amplified as some people struggled to understand our decision. Many people, who had also lived their entire lives under a bubble of similarity, saw little value in it. Some believed we were making a dangerous mistake riddled with grave consequences.

I understood this reluctance, having so recently identified with it. I was miles away from the growth I've since gained over time here. I had a lot to learn. But even in those early days in the neighborhood, I craved the complication of dissonance. The smallest seeds of curiosity were germinating, prompting me to ask new questions. *What am I missing out on? What if "the danger" has always been a myth?* Most staggering of all, *Do my new neighbors see me as their "other"?*

Basic Instructions for Seeing What's True

Our ability to relate with others is largely tied to our exposure. Because of systems put into place across time immemorial,[iii] most of us live sequestered from the wisdom and pure delight of those we've been told are not "like" us.

Though we can't always identify its source, homogeny is bred into our daily realities. It's hard to locate the problem in our categorized, cut-and-dried worlds. We stay quiet about our cravings, crawling into the void of the internet and Netflix, desperate to feel something and secretly wanting to be rattled.

We think we're the only ones.

All the while, the electric shock of humanity—that chaotic pop and jolt of different life experiences and new opportunities—is strung overhead, pole-to-pole. There's so much to gain from one another if we determine to lean in. It's time to trade the safe uniformity of AstroTurf for a pasture of wildflowers, thick with complications and sheer captivation.

Picture me giving you a gentle shove off the putting green and into the unpredictability of the life you're ready to *see*.

Acknowledge Our Blind Spots

First on the agenda is to take an honest look at our lives and acknowledge who's missing. This is humbling. The

iii. "Today's residential segregation in the North, South, Midwest, and West is not the unintended consequence of individual choices and of otherwise well-meaning law or regulation but of unhidden public policy that explicitly segregated every metropolitan area in the United States." From Richard Rothstein, *The Color of Law: A Forgotten History of How Our Government Segregated America* (New York: Liveright, 2017), vii–viii.

defensiveness rising up like emotional indigestion might compel us to fudge the numbers. Push through!

Here are a few questions to simplify the process:

1. Do you live in a place segregated by race?[iv] (Simply put: Do most of your neighbors look like you?)
2. Do most of the people in your inner circle express faith as you do? Vote as you do?
3. Have you ever invited someone of a different race or ethnicity into your home? Or been a guest in theirs?
4. Do you nurture honest relationships with those who qualify for government assistance? Those who fight addiction? People in the LGBTQ+ community? The disabled community? The chronically cranky person at the office? The sullen kid around the corner?

Once we notice who is not in our lives, we can begin to imagine what we, by default, are missing.

Just as dinnertime is made brighter and more interesting by plenty of salt and seasoning, regular life becomes richer and more complex when we regularly rub shoulders with those who have new things to teach us.

---

iv. For most Americans, the answer is yes. A *Washington Post* article explains that while the suburbs are gradually becoming more diverse, it's taking longer than anticipated, specifically due to factors like "money, preferences, and discrimination." The article also includes a feature to view the diversity index of your zip code. See Aaron Williams and Armand Emamdjomeh, "America Is More Diverse Than Ever—but Still Segregated," *Washington Post*, May 10, 2018, https://www.washingtonpost.com/graphics/2018/national/segregation-us-cities/.

Engage in Honest Self-Reflection

The next step is *not* to go shopping for friends to fill your missing categories. What we can do is awaken ourselves to new opportunities for connection and be ready to build authentic relationships over time.

If we want these fledging friendships to get off the ground, we need to get gut-level honest about our potential to cause damage even when our intentions feel flawless. After spending most of our lives surrounded by similarity, there's a lot we don't know about each other and plenty of wrong assumptions.

We are good people who want to be a part of making the world brighter for everyone. These facts don't exempt us from making a mess of things. The ground zero of humility, where we examine our faulty humanity and our decades of disregard, is the right posture for the road ahead. Let's don our reflective vests and proceed with caution.

Begin Our Reeducation

Moving through life with a new vision for connecting with people who aren't "like" us will yield fruit. When we exist in a default mode of searching for similarity, we are sure to find it. The same is true for the moment we expand our vision to seek what we've missed along the way. As new people emerge from the landscape, we'll ask ourselves how we didn't notice them before now.

No need to get hung up on this. The good news is, here they are! Here are the delightful humans we didn't know we were missing. They're here and we're here and it's all so exciting.

Now it's time to buckle down and do the work required.

Studying up on the cultures and complexities of those with different experiences means we're serious about drawing a wider circle of care. There's a lot we don't know or weren't taught, but we are adults with Wi-Fi access and library cards.

When I discovered our city is home to a large population of Spanish-speaking families, I got a bit overeager and signed up to take a Spanish class through the local parks department with high hopes of dusting the cobwebs off my geriatric high school Spanish.

I regret to inform you that to this day I remain dependent on a few clunky phrases and a handful of mostly unhelpful nouns. I can ask your name and offer you an apple, but beyond that it's a struggle.

While that tactic didn't provide the ease of connection for which I initially hoped, I remain persistently curious about Latine[v] culture, and I'm not just talking about considering the virtues of carne asada versus al pastor. It is of no great consequence to my neighbors that I happen to adore tacos. What unites us is the mutual resolve to hold one another in kind regard, learn the histories parceled out as trust grows, imagine the complexities, anticipate the hurdles, and notice the joys each of us carries.

v. Latino? Latinx? Hispanic? Terminology matters. I'm following the lead of Cuban American author and theologian Kat Armas and other similarly minded people. She writes, "The term *Latine* is used . . . to highlight the diversity of the Latino/a experience in gender, sexuality, nationality, place of birth, etc." Kat Armas, *Abuelita Faith: What Women on the Margins Teach Us about Wisdom, Persistence, and Strength* (Grand Rapids: Brazos Press, 2021), 191 fn 1.

Check Our Motives

As we trade our mirrors for windows, our sole objective should be a stronger, tighter community. That doesn't mean our junk won't still manage to creep in. Let's ask ourselves, over and over again,

Am I seeking connection and friendship with this person because I think I will somehow make their life better? Or do I truly believe they will brighten mine?

Does judgment or control line the walls of my intentions? Am I secretly hoping to put them on a better path (read: my path)? Am I trying to worm my way in to attempt to manage them in some way?

Am I willing to accept that my ways are not necessarily "best" and that I have a lot to learn from those with different ways?

Am I able to remain open?

Listen

Our most valuable skill as we move toward each other is our willingness to listen. That's all I'll say here, but it's so important I'm dedicating the next full chapter to this. See you in a few pages.

Join In

When we arrived in our new community and mostly out of some low-grade loneliness, Cory and I joined groups and meetings that were thriving long before we arrived. At PTO, our new church, neighborhood association meetings, and one special discussion group Cory affectionately refers to as "The Woke Grandpas," we found ready-made alliances with others near us. We also began supporting local shops, taquerias, and grocery stores. We jumped into the same places our neighbors were spending their time and cash.

Joining in rather than trying to build something new means being willing to show up as the newbie, which can ignite chronic shyness and introversion. Take heart. The path toward discomfort is the path of connection.

Be Normal

Take it from me: "normal" is easier said than done. I'm of the mind that God built us with brains because we are supposed to overthink absolutely everything. Leave no stone unturned! No possible awkward outcome left off the mental list that gridlocks us so we never leave our homes! No grand scheme left underruminated to the detriment of small, daily moments of contact!

When I'm able to step outside of my brain and fully engage in my body, the angst and confusion clear. No one is asking me to Do Something Amazing! (In fact, that idea alone smacks of the hidden agendas we just talked about.)

My task—my delight—is to embrace the life I've been given and to do some of that living out among the people.

Join me. We'll take walks and share food and race the clock for school pickup, awake and attentive, fully believing the greatest surprises arrive as we are simply being our actual selves.

Get Over Ourselves

Isn't it fascinating that while we crave authenticity and the grit of real life, the thing that so often holds us back is our fear of personal failure? We're far more gracious with the mistakes and awkwardness of others than our own.

Once in a while I have an interaction with someone where they fumble or reveal something unspectacular about themselves. Maybe they forget my name. Or they misplace their filter, say something *too* honest, and immediately apologize.

Maybe they even say the "wrong" thing to me and stumble to recover.

These glimpses of humanity draw me closer to them, not further away. It's one more assurance that I'm getting something raw and in-process, which eases the pressure. I exhale. Maybe perfection isn't a requirement for belonging, after all.

We are going to mess up, stick our feet in our mouths, and embarrass ourselves. Sometimes we'll be the ones bumbling through an awkward apology. We might hurt someone's feelings. We might forget our protective armor and show up more vulnerable than we intended.

Good for us!

It is in the risks we take anyway, along with the inevitable minidisasters, that we reveal ourselves as exactly human enough. We fling ourselves into the world, saying, "Yeah, me too."

Show Up Needy

We've been taught to be the ones with answers, opinions, and resources. We are the ones with the secret stash of butter, not the ones who scrounge for a stick when the temperature dips and the longing for chocolate chip cookies comes singing in our ears.

But there is nothing as disarming as swallowing that tough nut of pride and asking for help. We can be the ones who show up needy. Even if we're not accustomed to it.

I've asked for eggs, extension ladder loans, and someone to keep an eye on the kids in the backyard while I ran to pick up a sibling from practice. Once, in a dinnertime pinch, I knocked on my neighbor's door with an empty measuring cup in hand. Angel took it, ran back inside, and reemerged, smiling, to hand it back to me filled with glimmering vegetable oil.

Another time I sat down for a meeting at the coffeehouse in town and was suddenly panic-stricken that I'd left one of my stovetop burners on low. I sent out a frantic group text to four of my closest neighbors, asking if one of them could check. Heather ran to my rescue, finding my home in whatever state of "not meant for public consumption" it had surely been left in. She saved my day. But I hope she also learned that she could turn around and need me back.

Gifts along the Way

The big secret? Our motives will always be at least half selfish.

We've seen firsthand the ways our world is designed to keep us apart and indoctrinate us toward believing there's a "them." We've felt both the pang of loneliness that descends when we let ourselves be told who belongs to whom and the queasy understanding that we have been part of the problem.

And so we allow ourselves the treasure of hopeful curiosity, imagining what could be. The struggle to make each today better than each yesterday is a goal worthy of the common good.

But on the flip side of communal possibility, there are some perks in it for us too, which we can't help but acknowledge. More peace, more harmony, a greater sense of taking our citizenship seriously. Yeah. All of that.

Also actual *stuff*. Actual goodness and daily fun. There isn't a checklist titled "Things You'll Get When You Do This." It's more of an "Inherit Your Own Adventure" situation. My list is still in progress, ever-expanding. But here's part of it, for kicks.

Viva la Cuisine!

I credit my kids with this one. Specifically, my two Korean-born sons. As transracial adoptive parents, Cory and I have the responsibility to help them cultivate and preserve their cultural and ethnic identities. It would be unfair and damaging for us to expect them to assimilate into White American culture (whatever that even means).

They are fully American. And fully Asian. Though our appreciation and celebration of our differences should not end with enjoying the foods of these cultures, it remains a meaningful access point. Cal and Silas have given me the gifts of kimchi jjigae, samgyeopsal, japchae, and ddukbokki, to name a few of our favorites.

Similarly, I have enjoyed countless plates of fresh tamales and bowls of posole from Laura, homemade tres leches cake from Ana, and bowls of biryani and crispy pakoras from Asha. Once, a woman across town saw me out walking at 9:00 a.m. and handed me a piping-hot empanada straight off her oil-drum griddle.

Yard Party

In eight of the ten years we've lived here, we've celebrated the Fourth of July with our next-door neighbors. It started as an accident, two families out in our yards with a mutual awareness that joining festive forces is always the right choice.

In the years since, other neighbors have occasionally joined us. The more, the merrier! We heap our plates with burgers and homemade salsa. The kids race around the yards, turning small city lots into paradise found. The music rotates between pop, folk rock, and mariachi. Last year—I still don't understand how or why—we ended up listening to Alan Jackson's Christmas album on repeat. We swatted mosquitoes and lit Roman candles to "Holly Jolly Christmas." Somehow it all made sense.

Power in Numbers

Our corner of the block sits diagonal to a small city park. It's a popular spot for pickup soccer games and its playground is always crawling with kids. After noticing too many speeding cars on our street, several of us began to grumble about the need for a four-way stop at that intersection.

Mike, who had lived across the street for upwards of seventy years, thought we were wasting our time. According to him others had tried, though the details remain fuzzy. What I do know is that we decided to take *our* turn at trying. Short story long, three of us moms showed up to a city planning meeting to voice our concerns, and despite our skepticism that we had even been heard, a few weeks later I looked out my living room windows to see a crew of city workers installing a brand-new stop sign.

If I had to guess, I'd say it was Heather pushing her double stroller into that closet of a conference room that sealed the deal.

The moral of this story: there's strength in solidarity.

The moral of the bigger story? We don't seek a wider embrace of the world only because we think it's the right thing to do. We run after it because we know it's the trapdoor to the good life—samosas and party poppers included.

Mirror, Mirror

With any luck, we'll do the work of combing the uniformity from our lives in order to make space for people who stretch us. We need to be nudged into places where we feel awkward and unfit and prodded toward conversations where it's obvious we have much to learn. It is to our benefit that we locate small but meaningful ways to taste the discomfort of "outsider" status, acknowledging the people around us who have no other option.

But I would be remiss to not give a shout-out to old-timey friendships and bonds between like-minded people we meet along the way. (Sing it with me, Scouts: "Make new friends, but keep the old. One is silver and the other gold."[1])

If connection is the fabric of "us," what we're after is a tapestry dense with layers, a tight weave of acquaintances, neighbors, best friends, and familiar faces.

Here's a recent example. A handful of years ago, on a whim, Cory and I invited a dozen people from around town to our patio for snacks. Most of us were at least loosely familiar with each other. Everyone on the list was someone we hoped to get to know better. We found an opportunity to widen our web of local friendship and took it. Six people showed up.

We sat under the stars until 1:00 a.m., doing our best to cram the highlights of entire lives into a few hours. *It really worked.* I fell into bed that night beaming from the random wonder of it all.

Sealing our fate forevermore, we started a group Messenger thread dubbed "The 5th Street Phenoms," since three-fourths of us lived on the same street.[vi] The rest is history, including the part where I suggested a casual blood oath vow to never move away from each other.[vii]

The facts are that we're all White, middle-class, and married. We share similar evangelical upbringings and bear some of the same scars as we attempt to untangle our core

---

vi. Yes, it's corny. No, we don't care. Yes, I exclusively refer to us as such.

vii. I made this proposal within one week of that night on the patio. Friend-dating me can be intense.

beliefs around faith and worldview from those we inherited in childhood.[viii]

This friend group spans different life phases. Some of us have grown kids and grandchildren. Some hope for kids in the future. Some have chosen to not have children. We gather around spicy political issues and muse about who God is. We're united by the shared belief in a better world and the possibility of becoming better citizens.

The Girl Scouts never taught me which kind of friend was gold. There's no badge for that. Is it the old friends? Or the new? The friends "like us"? Or the ones we assumed were "different" until we got close enough to know better?

With great relief I can say that they all go into the soup of a well-layered life. There's room for everyone here.

Coming Home

We arrived home from our road trip the evening of Easter Sunday to find our neighborhood resurrected. After half a year of brutal cold and a year's worth of isolation, we were alive, baby.

I casually ignored my kids' inquiries about dinner, dropped my bags on the floor, and made a beeline straight to my garden. There was nothing growing yet. But the sun on my face helped me remember what soon would be.

Bibi spotted me from her garage, where she stood flip-

viii. Though this work doesn't necessarily lead to the change or abandonment of core beliefs, the process of examination is an important milestone, best met within a community where different perspectives are valued.

ping meat on a gas grill. "Come over!" she yelled. "Come for dinner!"

And so we did.

I grabbed an unopened bag of tortilla chips, stuck on the age-old American lie that we can never just receive.

We feasted on asada piled on freshly grilled tortillas with guacamole that made our eyes water. Miguel handed Cory a bottle of beer, and when that was empty, Cory ran inside our house and returned with two cans of his current favorite.

Bibi's mom sat quietly with us, laughing at the gestures that transcend language while trampoline springs squeaked from the side yard. City traffic and sizzling meat. An Easter hymn.

We talked about food and Chicago, marveled at how fast our kids were growing, laughed at Cory's low tolerance for spicy food, and loaded our plates with seconds.

Their teenage son showed up at the makeshift buffet with two other boys, each of them carrying a skateboard. "Hi," Bibi said to them. "Do you live nearby? Go ahead." She waved toward the food. "Help yourselves."

As late civil rights hero and US congressman John Lewis said, "We all live in the same house." He continued, "We all live on this little piece of real estate. It doesn't matter whether we are Black or White or Latino or Asian American or Native American. We are one people, we are one family, we are one house. And we must keep this house together. We must celebrate our diversity. We must preserve our diversity. All of us must be included."[2]

I am forced to reckon with the excuses I make to keep

distance between myself and those around me, or to try to show up to the world around me as need-less as possible. To continue to live by these patterns of toxic independence is to miss the magic of being alive together, in the same expansive house.

"I was hoping you would be back in time to eat with us. We didn't want to celebrate Easter alone," Bibi said to me as we ate together.

Later that night, Cory and I took a walk through the neighborhood, eager to reacquaint ourselves with the warm weather vibes that get buried every winter beneath wool sweaters and survival mode. Every block was hopping. We said hello to new faces and walked down alleys to the cadence of rap music and mariachi bands.

Circling back toward home, we ran into a neighbor wearing his pet python across his shoulders. Over the past years, our political and philosophical differences have sharpened into the typical tensions, maybe even divisions on our worst days. I did not opt to touch the snake, but in that bright spot of sun and kindness, I was reminded there's still plenty of overlap between us.

This is the sort of no-fuss, everyday acceptance so many of us are after. It's a song all its own, a rhythm of being sheltered and known, and we'd like to keep singing it.

Mutual trust and easy affection won't erase the ills of our wonky, wobbly world. We've got buckets of work to do, but beginning with a clear sense of solidarity is a great place to begin. Making one neighborhood more connected makes the world more connected. The math checks out.

Here's to inching away from the familiar.

Here's to trusting ourselves and each other more every day.

Here's to singing in the key of *us*.

ONE SIMPLE WAY
to Live as Neighbors

The next time you need help, ask for it. This is hands-down my favorite, most foolproof tip for building relationships with the people near you. As we are people taught to solve our own problems, this humble practice cuts to the heart of who we think we want to be. But remember, *interdependence* is the goal here. Independence is overrated, not to mention lonely. A world where we rely on each other is better, brighter, and safer.

Like everything else worth doing, it will take some practice. Start small. Run next door and ask if they'll grab your mail while you're gone for the weekend. Cross the hall and ask for an egg. Before running out to buy a small appliance or yard tool that won't get a lot of use, see if someone nearby has one you could borrow.

The best part? Though this isn't about keeping score, it can be fun to find creative ways to repay the favor. (I recommend a hefty slice of whatever you baked with that borrowed egg.) Showing up needy sets the tone for a life of ordinary connectedness. You go first, and others will follow. (I'm excited for you already!)

CHAPTER 3

Listening > Talking

We listen to the stories around us as a soundtrack for connection.

ONE OF MY FAVORITE MOMENTS of our Sunday church service is greeting time. When I was growing up, this routine was more like a mild form of interpersonal torture with forced handshakes and customary hellos between the same people week after week. It never felt sincere, like an icebreaker between people who were perfectly content keeping their distance.

St. Mark's United Methodist Church changed my opinion on this, particularly when the guys (and gals) from the neighborhood work release facility began showing up. They arrived unencumbered by the sleepy politeness that had marked most of my past experiences. What used to feel impersonal and almost pointless became rowdy and fun.

Given the signal, our cramped sanctuary would explode into commotion, with people crossing the aisles, trading hugs and high fives, doing what we could within a few minutes to actually get to know each other.

This collective enthusiasm mixed with an interesting rotation of newcomers to whittle away my old ideas about personal space. I started to view small talk as a starting point rather than mindless filler. If that sounds sort of magical, it's because it is. But that doesn't mean I'm particularly good at it or that my custom blend of relational deficiencies doesn't still muck things up a bit.

One recent Sunday I asked an unfamiliar man his name only to realize, moments after he told me, that I still had no earthly clue what it was. This happens to me often. How do I manage to forget someone's name three seconds after they share it? *Starts with a . . . T? Was it Tom? Todd? What is my problem? Why do I care enough to ask but not enough to actually listen to and mentally record the answer?*

I stared at my new "friend's" shaggy brown hair, kind eyes, nondescript T-shirt. *Tim? Terry?* Arlene took to the organ, hitting the opening notes of "Great Is Thy Faithfulness." I reflected on his name for all three verses. *Was it a J?*

As our culture continues to move at the speed of technology, it becomes more urgent than ever to consciously slow down and relearn how to listen. The strength of our bonds depends on it. Finding our way from passive hearing to active listening is the name of this game.

Spoiler alert: we need some practice.

The Facts on the Ground

Our collective humanity is at stake when we lean in to the comforting insulation of echo chambers. Finding mutual understanding with the people near us, from all walks of life, requires the lost art of *listening*.

Proximity is an excellent starting point, but sharing a zip code alone will not get us to a place of mutual trust and care, both of which are acts of wisdom and will. We excel at multitasking—to our detriment. Maybe it's just me, but too often I see "listening" as one more task to complete—one I can easily wrap around other items on my to-do list that seem more urgent or productive.

I run errands while listening to the news. I squeeze in current events podcasts while prepping dinner. I catch up on voice messages while tidying up or taking a walk. Even showering becomes a passive opportunity to DO MORE.

At least half the time, I realize I'm only half listening and couldn't repeat key details if my life depended on it. I rewind and try again, yet sometimes I still miss what I was trying to hear the second time. We can teach old dogs new tricks but I can't seem to teach myself that listening with my whole mind is a worthy investment.

Unless we commit to really listening, we won't experience the life we're looking for.

It's hard to imagine a time when learning to listen wasn't important. These days, it's a four-alarm emergency. We're like the frog in the pot unaware that it's about to be cooked. The temperature on civil discourse keeps inching up, degree-by-degree, but we don't exactly feel the heat. We just know it's basically always hot in here.

Simple disagreements feel calamitous so we avoid them. Or we try to shut them down by (verbal) force. Maybe we're afraid to enter in because we're worried we don't have the right words or command the right data. Many of us actively avoid conflict because it makes us anxious, an emotion that's uncomfortable and even terrifying. When the shadow of conflict hovers like dense fog, it's easy to see why we tend to peel away from those who aren't "on our team."

And all the while we're missing out. We're forgetting how to disagree well, how to learn from each other. We're forgetting we're all just human.

Becoming better listeners shortens the space between us and reminds us why listening matters in the first place. Unsurprisingly, mastery of this skill has humble roots. We learn to listen to each other by first engaging our bodies in the ordinary work of listening to our actual lives. Attentiveness 101, audio version.

Listening School—An Experiment

It's 6:45 p.m. on a run-of-the-mill summer weeknight and I'm sitting on the back patio. Here in northern Indiana, where the winters rage well into spring and we hibernate for half the year, I'm drawn outside into the heat and humidity whenever possible.[i]

---

i. Please don't hear this as "I am active." I'm shamelessly indoorsy at heart. I just prefer to take my energy (tranquil of body, intense of mind) into the great outdoors when possible.

Stilling myself, I carefully consider what I hear in this one moment in time: the basic and familiar treasures. There's a chorus of birds, four-part harmony on the choir risers of walnut, maple, and hackberry trees. Traffic heads north on Main Street, visible between Edgar's and Kent's houses. Big rigs barrel past, their wheels on pavement sounding strangely like ocean surf.

The dull *thunk* of a car hood slamming echoes through a neighborhood populated with fixer-uppers (one of which lives in my garage). I wonder whose hands are greasy this time. A song sung in Spanish perfumes the air, plaintive and low.

In the distance, the wail of a train—my most complicated neighbor by far—draws closer. That horn often means I'll be making an impromptu U-turn and showing up three minutes late. Sitting on the back porch with nowhere to be, I can afford to feel affection for it.

The shouts of kids playing at the park animate the summertime thrum. A teenager passes by, his voice simultaneously a giggle and a growl.

Skateboards on pavement. A garage door opening. The train coming closer, grinding against its steel rails.

Silas and Lizeth coast down the back alley on scooters while beetles feast on roses and locusts floss with my geraniums.

I'm getting sleepy.

From behind, I hear a voice. "Hi, Shannan!" Ashlyn, a young neighbor, turns my attention to the meat of the moment. She's asking, along with all of creation, *Are you here? Are you listening?*

Every choice to slow down and attend to what *is* with our whole selves is an invitation to belong more fully and engage more deeply with this life we've been given.

We are here. We are listening.

How to Actually Listen

Let's dump all of our popsicle sticks on the table and rebuild a vision for healthy, productive listening from the ground up. No stick or step is too small to reconsider.

Stop Talking

It is so hard for some of us to stop talking. (Raises hand.)

I have an inborn fondness for silence and the good fortune of a job that comes with many hours of sitting alone in my house. But every quiet writing day has its end, and if you happen to find me there, strap in for the ride. I've been married for over twenty years and I'm only now getting better at recognizing Cory's politely glazed-over look when I've droned on too long.

Further, I cannot tell you the number of times I've walked away from a conversation with the palpable, unforgiving awareness that I talked too much. I have so many words. My brain is good at synthesizing information but I'm constantly drafting mental notes and spinning off into new directions. I bear the compulsive urge to verbalize every riff. This is a fact of my life and there's no way to make it sound pretty or poetic.

Maybe your struggle is the opposite. You have to push

yourself to speak up. This is so foreign to me that I honestly don't know what to offer you, other than the sincere promise that I'm trying to make more space for your voice because we're all better for it. *Oh, to utter words more discriminately!*

Either way, if we want to get serious about listening, we need to leave room for other people to speak. Not every conversation has to be a verbal barrage (absolutely preaching to myself). We don't have to constantly instruct, debate, or fill the space. Let's learn to let the natural pauses ripen. Let's beware the danger of becoming walking white noise machines. Often the best thing we can do is just sit together and *be*.

Stillness is a brilliant teacher.

Slow Down

Second, we need to slow down.

I value downtime and do a decent job of keeping it in the rotation. This is not the part where I talk about the importance of rest or self-care (we'll get to that). This is an acknowledgment that the human job description comes with a good bit of commotion. We have places to be and things to do. No need to apologize for that.

But! We do need to keep our priorities in check. If our hope is to know and be known by the people near us, we need to protect the space between us.

This is what moving too fast looks like.

Exhibit A: after speaking out at a public meeting about a difficult and painful community conversation, I was invited to a meeting with a local leader who holds a great deal of power.

I was grateful.

The invitation seemed to indicate that I, and others who spoke up, had been heard. The risks seemed significant at the time, but perhaps they were worth it. Maybe change was on the horizon.

To my great disappointment, this person said the right things, such as "I have invited each of you to speak with me separately because I want to hear more," yet throughout our short time together he repeatedly glanced out the window and up at the clock.

He knew pursuing deeper conversation was the right thing to do but was unable or unwilling to slow down enough to actually listen. As frustrating as it was, I knew there had been times I'd been guilty of the same, checking the right boxes with the wrong heart.

If we say we want to listen, we need to be sure we mean it.

Exhibit B: my youngest child, Silas, has a high-octane energy source. (Lucky kid!) His body is constantly on the go. His mind operates in double time. He's always looking toward the next thing, always scheming. More often than not, his big ideas require parental participation, which can be a challenge for someone like me, whose energy reserves are primarily mental.

He recently wanted (needed!) my help with something and was prepared for me to once again try to stall his genius.

Me: "There's no rush. We'll get around to it. Life has just been busy."

Silas: "Okay, but does life *have* to be busy? Or was this an accident?"

I couldn't come up with a satisfying answer, even for myself.

Life doesn't have to be busy by accident. It can be full by intention. We get to set our pace without apology and decide who and what we slow down for.

Silas is one of the people I need to slow down for. That's a given. But the list needs to be longer than our nuclear family and best friends.

We're trying to knit a thicker, sturdier fabric. A blanket that covers more of us. Yet we cannot possibly slow down for every situation and moment life throws at us. We would drown in incidentals without a plan.

But it is worth asking ourselves, *Who do I want to hit the brakes for, on purpose? What might that look like?*

Quit Drafting Our Own Narrative

One of my bad habits is pretending to listen when I'm actually drafting my next response. On the outside I'm nodding along, punctuating conversation with the perfect amount of inviting nonverbals. *Exactly!*

On the inside I'm typing 100 wpm with my thumbs. I'm watching like a hawk for the slightest pause. I'm a wildcat ready to pounce. I'm a whole zoo. And I know my attempts at covering my tracks aren't as convincing as I hope.

Quelling this compulsion is more difficult than ever when absolutely everything feels urgently polarizing. It's all hot takes and *show me your data*. Across history, people have known the frustration of disagreeing about big and small things. This alone doesn't make us special. But right now the possibility of surviving our rival opinions with our relationships intact feels questionable.

This is the gravel in the skinned knees of our humanity. I don't know a surefire solution for something embedded so deeply.

But I'm hopeful that if enough of us push against it, civility might break through. Sitting down for coffee or trading thoughtful DMs with our "enemies," not to change each other or find total agreement but to really listen, has the power to corrode the iron will of our "opposing sides."

Imagine a conservative and a liberal sitting together and saying, "This is how I arrived here," over two steaming mugs. Who's to say this wouldn't be the butterfly effect leading to productive public discourse?

It probably wouldn't be easy. But we're sturdy, remember? We're hope-holders. World-changers. Back-havers.

We're not afraid.

Scratch that. We *are* afraid.

But we won't let that stop us.

Cultivate Curiosity + Wonder

The natural world leads us in the way of nuance. It illuminates our lack of control and highlights our smallness. The truths it tells are the backbeat of daily citizenship. If it can snow in May (it CAN), then maybe hope and justice and basic empathy don't hinge on data points. And if the tulips can survive the snow, if my blackberry canes still manage to bury us in fruit come August, maybe we can survive hard conversations spun from love.

It's a powerful thing to move through this world with our curiosity intact. I'm blindingly aware of when mine starts to break down. I retreat to the easier framework of black-and-white thinking. My way is Right. I replace every *and* with an *or*. I'm angrier. I have a harder edge. My shoulders relocate themselves up to ear level.

My opinions tend to be large and in charge. Gut instincts are often my guide and I don't sway easily. I prefer to at least *pretend* to have the facts and spit them out accordingly. Saying "I could be wrong," or "Have you thought of it from this perspective?" feels riskier than ever. Daring to say without shame "I don't know" feels like a welcome mat for criticism. Slowly, I'm learning that bulldozing my way to being "right" is often all wrong. The braver way is pausing to say, "Hmmm . . . tell me more."

Because the secret truth is we all camp some nights beneath the stars of the in-between.

Curiosity lights our way to compassion.

Remember What's True

So, here we are. We're quieting down, listening fully, carefully considering, willing to be wrong. We're committed to curiosity. Now what?

Now we get comfortable in tension.

This tension can be external (the conversation isn't going well, the divide suddenly seems impassable) or internal (we

CURIOSITY LIGHTS OUR WAY TO COMPASSION.

don't have clear opinions or answers in an age where we must know exactly how we feel at all times and be able to communicate it effectively).

Any of these might threaten to make us bolt.

But listening sets the intention that it is not primarily about us, even when someone is coming at us or applying a smackdown or pressing us to choose a side.

We are not meant to be everyone's teacher. We are not meant to be everyone's conscience. We are not meant to be everyone's priest.

I need this reminder on repeat. It comes in handy with everything from parenting clashes to raw conversations about sensitive issues.

If I'm feeling defensive, I need to remember it's not about me.

If I'm feeling pushy or controlling, I need to remember it's not about me.

If I'm feeling like running for the hills, never to return, I need to remember it's not about me.

Even if I'm simply feeling bored to tears, it helps to remember it's *not about me*.

Notice Who Is Missing

We can only really *know* those to whom we are listening. It often takes us time to realize certain voices *are* missing.

I'm a voracious reader, always plowing through several books at a time, the floor by my bed an abyss of novels and nonfiction. I've been this way since the dawn of time.

Several years ago I realized I was exclusively reading White authors. Across the board. It was suddenly so obvious; I was amazed I'd never recognized it before. So I set out to read more widely. In fact, I set the goal to read *mostly* authors of color. I was operating at a deficit and had a lot of catching up to do.

I grabbed titles about racial justice. I also dove into novels, memoirs, commentaries, cookbooks, and poetry written by people of color.

It changed me.

Absorbing different realities lit up the cobwebs of my consciousness and exposed my biases. I found the overlap. I noticed some of my mistakes and the gaps in my learning. I started to understand that healing asks us to chuck our shoes and wade into the murky waters of complicity and pain.

Listening to the voices at the edges—those furthest outside our own experiences with the least amount of power, those most vulnerable, those most directly affected by the conversation—will require us to challenge dominance, along with its gatekeepers and PR specialists. It will also open us up to a more nuanced perspective and make us more humble as we learn our way is not the only way.

We'll have to clear the decks in order to make room for new growth. This is about digging deeper, listening wider, and mining our curiosity.

Have a stare down with your bookshelves. Who do you see? Who is leading you? Teaching you? Shaping your world? If they largely remind you of yourself—or even if they just feel too familiar and cozy, not pushing against the realities of your own worldview—it's time to bust open the window and wave in some fresh air.

What Listening *Isn't*

Listening to each other, especially when we don't agree, is our yellow brick road toward constructive togetherness.

I wish it could go without saying that this doesn't diminish our need for healthy boundaries. There are times listening might put us in danger physically, emotionally, or spiritually. I'm not talking about having an endless stream of grace for nonsense or damaging rhetoric. We don't have to (and shouldn't) give oxygen to anything that seeks to cause harm (or even inflicts it under the guise of good intentions). It can be a beautiful thing to simply walk away.

Necessary disclaimers aside, including any I failed to mention, hearing one another is the sunshine and rain of understanding.

We've talked a good bit about what listening looks like. Here's what it doesn't look like:

- **Speaking.** Healthy, productive conversation has to be a mutual, taking-turns situation. When we're speaking, it's not our turn to listen. And if we're doing a lot of the speaking, we aren't listening enough.
- **Agreeing.** Listening does not equal endorsement. If we're afraid to listen to someone simply because

we don't see the world as they do, or we're nervous about what signals it might send, we only widen the chasm. We can listen *and* intensely disagree. We can listen *and* be heartbroken by what we hear.

- **Defending.** We can't fully listen and defend ourselves at the same time. End of discussion.
- **Being heard.** As we work on listening to understand, we are not guaranteed the other person is doing the same work. This is where boundaries might be needed. Though we are not promised a particular outcome, we can model good practices even if we do so alone.

The Conversation We Can't Afford to Ignore

As I write, the national conversation over anti-racism looms large. Regardless of where we happen to sit, we hear alarm bells.

The fact that our armpits might now be spontaneously sweating highlights our need to think more clearly about what it means to listen well and not turn away when things start to feel complicated.

This conversation is an inflection point of our day. Though upholding the full dignity of everyone and fighting for equity certainly has political implications, it should not be a partisan issue. This affects all of us. The hope for genuine healing will require everyone. As Bernice King, daughter of Martin Luther King Jr., said, "If you're not working for justice, stop calling for peace."[1]

I am not an anti-racism expert. I'm a White woman committed to learning, filling in the gaps, and doing better. Listening to the experiences of people of color is my only way through.

Our choices will either deepen the divide or bridge the gap. In the words of poet laureate Amanda Gorman, "Being American is more than a pride we inherit, it's the past we step into and how we repair it."[2]

The shovel is in our hands. Will we use it to dig the divide or to build a bridge?

Day One

For some of us, today is Day One of choosing to engage rather than avoid this conversation.

As the mom of four non-White kids, I wish I could say my Day One was the moment I first held one of them in my arms. In reality it was many years later, when our oldest son, Robert, became a part of our family. At the time he was barely nineteen years old and headed to prison. After serving nine months, he came home wearing an ankle monitor and moved into the basement bedroom. (On weekends, his twin one-year-olds moved in too.)

Watching him battle through life as a young Black man was my crash course on all I didn't know about the enduring stain of racism across America. Week after week, year after year, we've seen him try to wrestle his way out of a system that relentlessly keeps him pinned to the mat.

I've been there in the courtrooms and been patted down for prison visits with my pockets stuffed with quarters to buy him a cheeseburger from the vending machines. I've sat in the passenger seat of his car as an officer does a U-turn on Main Street to follow us for a mile. Later, after he had been pulled over four times in the same weekend for engaging his turn signal too late, I sat in a musty room with city officials and demanded an explanation. (The explanation? "We operate on our hunches." The truth? Their hunches were wrong.)

It is brutal to watch your child spend so much time, energy, and money trying not to break beneath the weight of this unfair world.

Of course, our younger kids matter just as much as Robert. His experience is not more compelling or meaningful than theirs. But at the time they were little and, in many ways, still protected from the world.

Watching him move through the world hypervisible and overpoliced, a target for hundreds of years of embedded racism and violent assumptions, jolted me awake from my lifelong doze.

Becoming his mom changed me.

As my younger kids get older, I have a devastating front-row seat to the ways they, too, are subjected to racism. I'm achingly aware that teaching their mom by example is too heavy a burden. I'm also constantly worried that other people like me[ii] might never "get there" without a similar secondhand experience.

ii. White, middle class, moving through my entire life with relative ease and readily available oblivion.

I get impatient. I want to speed things up, to onboard more of us into the conversation, to build our resilience so that we're better equipped to speak up.

Silence Is Compliance

Some people suggest that to merely bring up the reality of race and racism is to create division. This is a classic "nice" way to shut down vital conversation, sidestepping our culture toward the false and damaging ethos of color-blindness. If we pretend we don't "see" race in the first place, how do we expect to see (and repair) the racism caused by our differences?

Insulated from the negative outcomes, we can find it easy to believe we might be better off staying in our corners and pretending everything is fine. Avoiding discussions can seem healthier than potential hostility and hurt feelings. All the while, entire communities are crying out, "Things are not fine!" Our silence is not benign.

In reality, silence is complicity. Martin Luther King Jr. said, "In the end, we will remember not the words of our enemies, but the silence of our friends."[3]

The real question is discerning when to speak up and when to hush up. Will speaking up cause tension? Would we rather avoid it? It's okay to be honest with ourselves and confront our fears. As Emily P. Freeman said, "When I am silent, may it be because I'm learning and listening and not because I'm afraid."[4]

Though these conversations can get messy, even fiery, we need them. They require a lot of everyone involved, particularly people of color—whose experiences of trauma can become fodder for our education if we aren't careful. This can be a common mistake in our zeal to make up for lost time, but our friends, family, coworkers, and neighbors of color do not owe us this. Rather than imposing this labor on them, we should look to paid professionals and published resources.

Thankfully, many have chosen to take up this work. Bridge-builder and anti-racism educator Latasha Morrison sums up the beginning tasks of White people on the road to growth:

1. Don't deflect racism.
2. Don't defend racism.
3. Don't deny racism.[5]

As we hope for a more just world, may we embrace the words of artist and designer Cami Zea: "You are my neighbor and I commit myself to seeing your humanity first, then asking questions later. You are my neighbor and I am here to care for you in ways that are tangible and loud."[6]

Listening is the price of admission for a stable world, especially if the thought of it makes us feel antsy, guilty, or scared. The fruit will not grow overnight. This is long-haul work. The shifts are sure to feel sluggish.

Success might show up quiet and small, in hard conversations that last ten minutes longer this time before the inevitable breakdown. Maybe we'll speak up where we once would've let things slide. Our mom or our childhood best friend or our surliest coworker might look us in the eye and say they're starting to get it.

Racism won't meet its end because we crack the code or utter the perfect combination of words to permeate the souls of humankind. It will end because we slow down and listen to people of color, historians, journalists, and those whose experiences we can't even imagine. We will listen to the voice inside us screaming, *This is not right!* and to the part of us that *knows* we've contributed to the problem.

We will listen when it's hardest. When we feel most vulnerable. We'll push ourselves to keep listening even after we worry we've met our limit, recognizing that to tap out is a privilege in itself. We will believe in the power of humility, staving off the urge to deflect or overexplain or justify—and we will keep on listening.

Hearing makes us more human.

Learning to listen makes us revolutionaries.

Tea for Two, with a Side of Humility

The real work of listening is not all rainbows and sunbeams. It's taxing. Humbling. Opportunities for growth present themselves, inconveniently, when our emotions are running hot and the last thing we want to do is surrender. Yet it's in the moments when we feel justified in our certainty, or even our anger, that we have the most to learn.

(Ask me how I know.)

One morning, my family woke up to a moderate tragedy

involving a beloved pet. I held it together through their tears and got them to school one breath before the tardy bell. Thanks to this unforeseen disruption in our morning, I was now running late for an appointment that had been scheduled for weeks, a gift from my sister intended as a stress reliever.

The railroad crossing arms descended just as I approached the tracks, cementing my fate. By the time I arrived, a smooth seven minutes late, I was hanging on by a thread.

I did my best to shake it off. Here I was! My day was about to improve!

The person who met me at the door apparently hadn't received the improvement plan and instead told me what I already knew: I was late. It was an inconvenience to everyone. Etcetera.

I opened my mouth to defend myself but spontaneously started crying instead.[iii] I eked out a few sad words about my morning, my kids, our pet. I probably mentioned the train, because why not? Then I turned and stomped out the door, my cheeks burning with several layers of anger, shame, and embarrassment.

During the short drive back home, my sadness reconstituted into anger, shielding me from the vulnerability of my truer emotion. (Classic me.)

When the owner called to get my side of the story, I was ready. I shared my experience.

She defended her employee.

I doubled down. She did the same.

---

iii. Crying in front of people happens to be one of my least favorite activities.

I felt my biting reaction was justified. (I'm sure she felt the same.)

The trouble was, nothing had been resolved. We were still a couple of mad hens, brooding in our separate corners. As my emotional responses regulated, I realized I had earned my first official enemy in a city that feels more like a small town. There was no way I could avoid her forever.

Warranted or not, she had seen the worst of me. The thought made me sick.

When obsessing over our dustup didn't solve anything, I looked her up on Facebook. Surprise, surprise, we had quite a bit in common. This complicated things.

I couldn't shake her. I couldn't figure out, once and for all, which one of us had been right. After more deliberation and consternation, I sent a hesitant DM into the ether, asking if she would be willing to meet for coffee. She said yes, adding that she had recently bought my book and was reading it. (It seems we were mutually intrigued and/or beleaguered.)

When we met, conversation flowed easily at the little wooden table (both of us drinking a London fog latte, of all things.) She saw me in ways that were surprising and comforting.

We didn't waste time hashing out our bygones. We simply listened to each other as humans. There's no adorable bow tied around this story. We didn't become buddies. But we did clear the air, choosing to see each other as fully human and in need of care in a world that bangs us around.

When we see ourselves as woven into the same fabric,

one enemy is one too many. Working toward repair and shared understanding is always worth it.

My path occasionally crosses with hers around town. When this happens, I hope she and I always remember the time we were given the chance to dislike each other from a safe distance—but chose otherwise.

A Chorus of Connection

Half of my kids play in the orchestra at school. One violin. One cello. Several times a year, we get the opportunity to see them in concert. As someone not particularly musical, I'm in awe every time. There's something fancy about orchestras, even those comprised solely of seventh graders who show up—again—wearing white socks with their black concert shoes.

As time passes the Martin musicians continue to grow in their art. The pieces get longer and more complex. They start moving more with the music, sailing on the current they create. I love it all.

But my favorite part is the fifteen seconds before a show begins. Each musician sits in their chair, testing their bow and strings, tuning their instrument. They're playing different notes at different tempos, but they're playing with conviction.

Soon everything will come together.

But first it's a cacophony. Musical chaos.

Then there's the pause.

They sit a little straighter. The conductor's baton lifts.

The chaos converges into a unified song.

We can't have the symphony without first having the dissonance.

When I'm emotionally healthy enough to locate hope in the soup of humanity, I'm inclined to believe it arrives not as a monologue but as a song. You'll sing your part. I'll sing mine. With time and persistence, our notes will build and blend into something beautiful.

Here's to being quiet enough to listen, awake enough to see, curious enough to hope, and bold enough to believe it's our business.

ONE SIMPLE WAY
to Live as Neighbors

In the context of my beloved place, the south end of our block holds my strongest ties. I've made it my mission to know the names and faces of the people who live in the seven houses closest to us. (At least two of these are inhabited by people who prefer to keep their distance. Honoring that preference is our way of loving them.) Though our relationships vary, there's something special about knowing, on even the most basic level, who we are. As people come and go, I've learned to get scary-intentional. I no longer leave it up to my scattered memory. Now I track them via an email sent to myself, titled (you guessed it) "Neighbors."

If you've lived in your place for a long time and worry it's too late to expose what you should know, take a deep breath, walk over with a snack to soften the blow, and simply begin by saying, "I'm sorry, I should know this by now." They won't think you're strange. They'll think you care.

Afterward, race home and write it all down. You're one step closer.

CHAPTER 4

Open Door >
Perfect Décor

We invite others in, seeking to connect, not impress.

RECENTLY, THROUGH A FORTUITOUS CHAIN of events, I met a new friend, Rai, and bonded with her instantly over a shared ride to the airport after an event. Over the course of the fastest hour of my life, we talked nonstop, barely coming up for air. Though I wasn't keen on missing my flight (and actually have a pretty notorious history of broad-spectrum airport woes), as I sat in the passenger seat I watched our arrival time on her map tick down, dreading the moment she'd pull up to the curb and deliver me to the friendly skies.

How did Rai already feel like a trusted friend? Would I ever see her again? Was she feeling the same way? (I hadn't been on a first date in over twenty-five years but the feelings were familiar. Forging new friendships in adulthood is high stakes business.)

We snapped an obligatory selfie at the curb and then she drove away.

I introduced her to the Voxer app and, across several states and hundreds of miles, the conversation between us that began in her rental car continued. A couple months later, in the spirit of our match-made-in-friend-heaven, we took a quick trip together to seal the deal. Soon after she sent me a message:

> I can't wait to have you in my home, one day. And to visit yours. I don't think we know someone fully until we've been inside their home.

Being invited into someone's home is an honor. It's trust on a silver platter (or paper plate). Out in the world we're armed with protective gear, strategies for projecting a certain image or obscuring facts that feel like flaws. Our homes aren't as easy to contain. They tell other sides of the story, ready or not.

We enjoy visiting the homes of others but hesitate to invite others into ours. We want to really know the people in our lives but fear being fully known. This is the tug and pull of hospitality. Like so many of our tenets for connection, we long for it and simultaneously avoid it.

I've always found the word *hospitality* fussy, but I haven't discovered a decent replacement. It derives from the merging of two Greek words that translate *love* and *stranger*. To practice hospitality means, quite literally, to love strangers.

It's meant to go deeper than inviting immediate family over or hosting birthday parties a couple times a year. The word itself implies a decent bit of trust and surrender.

What we need is to reframe hospitality, to form a different way of thinking about it—one that takes the pressure off.

A man in Ecuador once pulled aside the pink flowered curtain at the entrance of his family's home and welcomed me inside. "Our home is humble, but our door is always open," he said.

Those are our goals.

Humble.

Open.

Love the Home You're With

Between our insecurities, our packed schedules, the added pressures of social media, and the trend toward cheese boards the size of kiddie pools, we've found ourselves in a crisis of welcome.

Recently, before the water for my morning tea had even boiled, I opened Instagram to an image so striking all I could do was stare. At its center was a dining table with a single candle casting its glow. Draped over the window behind it, a swag of lights twinkled against the dark chill of a winter evening. The walls were an inky black, an intriguing option for anyone but especially for a white-wall apologist such as myself. I was captivated by the cozy warmth. I zoomed in on the artwork, admired the wreath-adorned mirror, and imagined how my life might level up if a cut-crystal decanter was always within my reach.

I examined every facet of that room, a jaw-dropping mash-up of accessibility and elegance, then tapped the little airplane icon and shared it to my Stories with the caption, "I want my next meal around someone else's table to be right here."[i] A better alternative? "I'd love to sit at this stunning table one day!" The difference is small but meaningful.

I wasn't trying to change the world with my quippy version of a sincere compliment. But just as mountains are moved by the drip of melting ice and atmospheres shift by the tenth of a degree, our perceptions of ourselves and others, of acceptability and worthiness, are shaped by the quiet consciousness of what we consume.

When it comes to social media in this digital age, we know our part. Celebration. Inspiration. Aspiration. Drip by drip, tap by tap, we renew the contract, dotting our i's with tiny red hearts.

Through the filtered glow of social media we imagine who we—and our homes—*could* be.

I don't want to be too hard on Sister Instagram. I hang out with her almost every day. She brings the party—joy, solidarity, a new recipe for cacio y pepe, clever memes for miles, gorgeous rooms designed by thoughtful creators who help me see my home and even my place in this world in a different light.

But if we're not vigilant, she'll make us believe our job is

i. Follow @allthingsonatural for the gorgeous dining room but stay for the masterful, gracious way she creates conversations around themes of design, justice, joy, equity, rest, faith, and, *yes*, hospitality.

to buy more stuff and twist our identities toward the sunniest window where the lighting is always best. She'll have us thinking the goal is to make ourselves seem better than we are—that we won't be accepted as is.

Or maybe, say, on a regular Tuesday morning, someone you trust (like me) puts an image of a magazine-moody dining room in front of you and says that's where she wants to eat her next meal. Nine days out of ten, you nod along, scroll past, click over to follow the account, or feel the electric *ping!* of inspiration.

But what about the tenth day? That's the one that lodges a seed of self-protection in your soul: *What I have is not good enough.* Over time, it sends out new roots, unseen, that can grow into *I am not good enough.* The problem is *not* the art itself. I love all things home and have an Instagram feed that proves it.

The trouble arrives when we allow someone else's art to mangle our contentment or self-worth despite knowing what we see is all by design. Social media puppet masters bank on us seeing ourselves as lacking or less-than so we'll buy more of what's being hustled. *Your hair won't do the perfect beach wave? Try this new shampoo. Your living room isn't curated and picture-worthy? This life-changing sofa will put you on the right path.*

At this very moment, I opened Instagram to test the advertising algorithm. In a quick five-minute scroll, it tried to sell me a new wallet, a winter coat for a dog I don't have (??), a "shacket" (???), and a toy that promised to lure my kids away from screens and video games.

Friends, I bought the toy. I went to the app to scoff at how dumb they must think we all are and I BOUGHT THE TOY.

We are not immune to this nonsense.

This nonstop pressure for improvement and upgrades is partly to blame for why it can feel so threatening to open our door to others. We're afraid to be exposed as deeply ordinary and far messier than we'd like to admit, no matter where we fall on the home décor spectrum. Our Goodwill curtains aren't on-trend. Nothing matches. Our sofa is propped up at one end with a stack of books. Continually confronted with "evidence" that everyone else has it "more together," we slip into the destructive belief that for us, community does not require the vulnerability of sharing our physical space. We carve out our loopholes. *We don't need it! We're introverts! We're fine!*

We tell ourselves it's better this way.

The only thing left to do is flip the dead bolt.

I'd like to pause a moment to clarify the difference between hospitality and entertaining. What does it mean to open our homes to others? It is to be human, together, with the lights on.

A home is not a reflection of identity. It's a shelter for belonging through every season. I hope you're exhaling, because this is very good news. It means the pressure is off to shove parts of ourselves into the spare room and slam the door shut.

If we want to be known, *really* known, we're going to have to pull back the curtain and wave people in. Which means getting over the idea that our homes are here to perform on our behalf.

My friend Kristen lamented, "So much about hospitality is about entertaining. Not only do I have to feed you, but I have to do a dance? A limerick? A soliloquy? *What?*"

Haven't we all felt this way?

No doubt, my neighbors could write some killer limericks. But the goal is to lay down our defenses and be ourselves. It's time to throw our ideas about trying to impress out with the recycling and settle in together, just as we are.

What Living Really Looks Like

When it comes to hospitality, we seem to be divided among two separate camps. Half of us see our homes as primarily practical. They meet our needs and offer us comfort but are nothing like the homes on the internet, and we're afraid they aren't "company worthy." Hospitality feels overwhelming and we don't want to be judged, so we don't bother. Outside our smallest, most trusted circle, we decide we weren't cut out for that sort of thing.

The other half of us enjoy fluffing and sprucing and arranging. Consequently, we tend to warp hospitality from the opposite direction. We think everything has to be perfect. We're scared of shattering the perception that we have it all together. We might be a bit more inclined to host, but when we do it's with a lean toward impressing our guests. Not only is this exhausting but it's also an impossible bar to set for ourselves (and others). We walk away fixated on the one thing that didn't go right or realize at the end of the evening that we missed the funniest jokes and best conversations because we were so busy or distracted.

Either way, this is a misplaced issue of identity. Yes, our homes are deeply personal. When we let someone in, we *are* inviting them to see more of who we are. They are an extension of us—but they don't define us.

I once asked this question on an Instagram post: "What's stopping you from inviting someone into your home for a meal?" The responses ranged from, "I want the house to look perfect. I need to get over that!" to "A deep fear that no one will say yes to the invitation." A few people said that just reading the question made them cry. Summarizing the whole shebang, one woman wrote, "The practice of spontaneous community is so beautiful. But strangely, it is an internal struggle also."

We're all over the place. But one thing we have in common is that we're drawn to it and want to find a better path forward. We want hospitality to be a rhythm of life, not a pipe dream or cause for hives.

Just as going to church, the gym, or a favorite restaurant might be part of our weekly rhythm, we can hold the expectation that most weeks, someone other than our family will enter our home.

This intention would go a long way toward recalibrating our ideas of the acceptability—even our ownership—of our homes. That's what it did for me. When I got serious about inviting people in, clearing out all the clutter and polishing all the surfaces became unsustainable. As Cory reminds me when I lament the perpetual mess, "People *live* here."

Sometimes the tipping point into scrappier, on-the-fly hospitality is being willing to go first. Knowing very little about kinesiology or physical education of any kind, I hold on to hope that being hospitable is a bit like building muscle memory. Repeat, repeat, do it again—until it's a reflex.

When I started to let go of my urge to appear more presentable, absolutely no one cared. In fact, I began paying more attention to how I felt when I entered someone else's blissfully lived-in home: I relaxed. The pressure was officially off. I felt trusted, like a true insider.

My days include a constant rotation of dirty dishes. People eat here.

It includes unmade beds. People sleep here.

It includes messy stacks of books, artistic works-in-progress, unfinished projects, and jumbles of electronic cords. People learn here. People create here. People relax here.

People live here.

Not Dreading the Drop-By

I grew up in a family where "dropping by" unannounced was commonplace. What seemed normal in childhood became horrifying in adulthood. I didn't want to be taken off guard or found unprepared, nor did I want to put anyone else in that position.

I've started to see the flaws in this. As our culture goads

us toward autonomy and independence, our homes get incrementally quieter. We've become a culture defined by "personal space." Personal everything, really. The longer this continues, the more we come to see sharing our space as intrusive. We're nostalgic for close ties yet we uphold the silent agendas that keep our relationships locked in detachment. We fear the thing we want.[ii]

As I write this, we are in the phase of the COVID-19 pandemic where people are getting vaccinated and life is creeping back toward normalcy. Earlier in the week, after a year with very little action inside our home, some friends stopped by around 9:00 p.m. "We were at Dairy Queen and thought we'd say hi," they said. We'd just returned from Cal's baseball game; I was standing at the island amid a sea of dirty dishes, piled-up projects, and junk mail, eating a bowl of microwaved spaghetti. The house was in its general weeknight disarray, not a state I would have traditionally seen as "company worthy."

They declined my offer of reheated spaghetti but accepted a glass of water. We sat down at the table, pushing the messes out of the way. Within minutes we'd launched into a conversation topic deeper than the hour and circumstances could properly sustain. At one point, our friend Jason grabbed a tangerine from the basket on the table, wandered over to the silverware drawer and fiddled around,

ii. On a positive note, as America grows more racially and ethnically diverse, the trend away from multigenerational living is reversing to rates not seen since the 1950s. We're heading in the right direction, and our neighbors are leading the way. See D'vera Cohn and Jeffrey S. Passel, "A Record 64 Million Americans Live in Multigenerational Households," Pew Research Center, April 5, 2018, https://www.pewresearch.org/fact-tank/2018/04/05/a-record-64-million-americans-live-in-multigenerational-households/.

then sat back down with a fork, which he used to pry off the peel, a procedure I had never before witnessed. The easy, spur-of-the-moment, nothing-required-but-presence vibe was a comfort I realized I'd been craving.

This story might be your living nightmare. It once would have been mine. But I think most of us secretly wish for the sort of old-timey friendships that soften the blunt edges of a world that works to keep us distant and wary. It thrilled me that they thought of us and just showed up. I didn't need proof that we're in this together for the long haul, but it arrived anyway.

The point isn't that we should start crashing people's houses after dark. It's that we might reorient ourselves to a better, healthier, more connected way of life if we regain some chill about this sort of thing.

Having Said That

We're here for the über-practical, so let's talk about the realities of welcome. Despite all my talk, I do prefer to tame the Martin cyclone when possible.

For the sake of the nitty-gritty, I'm going to walk you through my typical MO.

1. I am a rabid floor-sweeper. The first time my friend Megan came to visit, she was legitimately shaken by how often I swept, and she teases me about it to this day. The walls can be falling down around me, but if my kitchen floor is clean I'm confident it'll all be okay. Most of us have one control-freakish quirk that requires our vigilance and always will. If I know

people are coming over, the first thing I do is sweep the floor. (Again.)

2. The next thing I turn my attention to is the main-level bathroom. I hate cleaning the bathroom, which means it always needs to be done. But if having company over requires a whole bathroom deep-clean, I'll be less likely to have company over. The goal here is to make things easier. Eyes on the prize! Here's my three-minute attack plan: wipe down the sink, mindful of crusted toothpaste globs and stray hair, paying no attention to the mirror. (Dirty mirrors are charming, right?) Quickly wipe down the grossest parts of the toilet (you know the ones). I'm not worried about dust on the lid of the tank. Dust builds empathy. If the trash can is more than half full, I empty it. I pull the shower curtain closed (not every secret needs to be told) and replace the hand towel with a clean one.

3. I move the precariously tall stack of vaguely important paperwork from the kitchen island and/or table to my bed. I then close the bedroom door.

That's it.

That's the whole plan.

If I have time or there happens to be a stray kid wandering about, I'll enlist them to "tidy up" the living room, which usually means wadding up the throw blankets and shoving them in the corner.

I almost always have dirty dishes in my sink. Dirty dishes are the tie that binds.

Tangled in the Weeds

Kendall, a friend I made on the internet, emailed me saying she would be passing through the area. Could she stop by for a visit? Resisting the immediate urge to overthink it, I replied to her email, "Yes, please stop by! I'm not sure how long you'll be around, but you are welcome to stay with us. We don't have an awesome guest room to offer, but we love to make room for friends."

She arrived on a typically busy weeknight for a family of teenagers and preteens. I managed to throw a shoddy version of taco bowls on the table. Our meal felt rushed. The beans came from a can and the plates were wildly uncute. All this for a talented baker who had just written a book about the power of sharing food. Between bites and conversation, I did my best to outrun my hunch that she was gravely disappointed.

And then it got worse.

After dinner, I showed Kendall to her temporary digs: Ruby's bedroom at the far end of our unfinished, work-in-progress basement. The good news? We were in the process of putting in a bathroom, which meant she wouldn't have to traipse upstairs in the middle of the night to share ours. The bad news? There was a toilet and tub but no sink yet. (Details!) I handed her some fresh towels and a bottle of soap, hoping she was willing to kneel by the tub to wash her hands and brush her teeth. (She was.)

Young adult me was screaming at who I'd allowed myself to become in middle age. These things were supposed to improve over time!

What I continue to learn from the people near me is that the way forward is often down. In the soil of authentic, come-as-we-are community, growth generally does not look like getting ahead. The goal is not to outpace or outshine.

My favorite home sage, Myquillyn Smith (aka the Nester), says, "The size of your house doesn't dictate the size of your hospitality."[1]

Tangled in the weeds of our limitations—things we wish we could change about ourselves or our home, the ideas we can't quite surrender—we rediscover our authentic identities as imperfect humans, doing our best and choosing to believe it's enough.

We are human, with messes, crusty dishes, hurt feelings, and hot takes. We are tired and busy and *alive*.

We are human, with dirty hair and ambiguous longings. We have questions that balloon into fears and fears that spiral into loneliness.

We are human, and when we're lucky, our homes remind us of what is true and good. And when we're the luckiest, we remind each other.

What Raspberries Teach Us

The velvety dining room of my dreams will not, in fact, be the next place I share a meal. Sometime soon I will find a seat in a kitchen nearby. Some of these spaces in my neighborhood would wow you with their good design sense or crafty ingenuity. Some are the sort of cozy that calls me back to my own childhood, as warm and unfussy as buttered toast. Some don't have a table to speak of.

The last table I sat at was in our new neighbor's garage for their daughter's first birthday. My cheeks flushed when I realized we'd showed up underdressed, though no one seemed to mind. I watched as two men hoisted a piñata from the rafters and laughed as the kids took turns whacking it. When the guests lined up to take turns holding the baby and we smiled from our seats, the obvious outliers in a party packed with bloodlines and old friends, they pulled us up front, placed her in our arms, and took pictures as though we were family.

Our homes might be where we experience the freedom to live the truest version of ourselves. But they are not *who* we are. Some of us create art with a side table and a pitcher of weeds. Some of us don't imagine why anyone would go to the trouble. Some of us feel shy about the condition of our homes. Some of us only wish we had a home to call our own.

In the end, I'm not so sure any of our homes were ever meant to be "our own." We seek refuge in this world, physical structures to shield us from the elements, warm caves of privacy where we rest, retreat, and search for missing socks. Our homes are meant to shelter us, but they never truly will until they shelter others too.

At their best our homes are harbors, not hideaways.

I once read about a fancy woman who placed bowls of fresh raspberries throughout her home as a "better alternative" to candy. I thought of the expense of even the smallest plastic box of supermarket raspberries, and I remembered a friend who once sat at my island and admitted she had never tried raspberries. Apples, grapes, strawberries? Sure. Raspberries were a bit more unfamiliar and never in her budget.

For me, raspberries symbolize luxury, a rare treat, scant and in demand. More than once I've splurged on a container only to leave them languishing in the fridge because I loved them too much. They're too special to be gobbled up over the sink during a quick workday lunch. The moment has to be perfect. A whole mood. I hover, a guardian of their extravagance, warning everyone not to touch. "I'm saving them for something!" I insist.

Meanwhile they rot.

This warning also applies to our homes. If we allow ourselves to become scared or think our space is too precious, one of our greatest sources of mutual comfort and protection will rot around us, underused. As my friend Myron said, "Our homes can only keep us so warm and so dry." Beyond that, they're also meant to bring us together.

We don't need *more* or *better*. What we need is each other. The pile of shoes on the rug by the door. The winter coats heaped up on the bed. We need everyone congregating in the kitchen, the cackling, and the five different side conversations drowning out the playlist. We need the clanking of dishes, the inevitable spills, the kids veiling their tattling as "reporting." We need to know for sure we're safe and loved in more than one space. Isn't that the expression of home we can't get enough of?

Our son Robert lived with us for a couple of years, but after he'd moved into his own place he showed up late one night, unexpectedly. "I got lost," he said, slightly bewildered. "I don't know how it happened, but my map was glitching and I couldn't figure out which way to go. The only place I knew how to get to was home. And I knew once I got here, I wouldn't be lost anymore."

Sharing our homes is like breaking off a piece of ourselves and passing it around, a true offering of just-as-we-are acceptance. The good life awaits—that messy, last-minute, grab-your-own-fork kind.

But only if we're willing to trust that all good things are best when shared.

ONE SIMPLE WAY
to Live as Neighbors

Invite someone over! A neighbor. A new friend. Resolve to let it be real, not perfect. It doesn't have to be a dinner or even at night. It could be a last-minute, "Come roll your eyes at *The Bachelor* with me!" Or a simple, sincere, "I want to see your face!"

If you find yourself feeling bad about the state of your home or what you have compared to others, nothing makes us fall in love with our kitchens and living rooms like sharing them. Or if that feels like too much right now, ask someone to meet you for a cup of coffee or a walk-and-talk.

Swipe on some ChapStick, open a bag of chips—wherever you are, take a step forward and let it be enough.

CHAPTER 5

Familiar > Fussy

> We serve tacos and pizza like the feasts they are,
> because fancy is overrated.

NOW THAT WE'VE MADE PEACE with the vital practice of welcoming people into our truest selves by inviting them into our homes, the next question is obvious.

What on earth should we feed them?

At its core, the idea of real-life connection, with all of its risks and rewards, will continue to push and pull us. We're drawn toward a rhythm of togetherness, but as we inch closer to the living, breathing reality, what sounded downright melodic from a safe distance now sounds a bit more like carnival music: optimistic enough, but we can't help but wonder if something's about to jump out and scare us.

If it's not already clear, barriers to relationship lurk everywhere, because we've accepted a system that paints the whole thing as a contest. By passively accepting this as status quo, we've been complicit in the decline of practical togetherness.

Growing up, the word I heard for this was *fellowship*. It's a churchy word that, as far as I could tell, boiled down to "a group of people eating together while the adults laugh a lot and the kids run wild." Any natural "fellowshipping" instincts I have were embedded into my consciousness during childhood. I'm not sure what special sauce my parents and their friends managed to concoct, but they built and sustained a rhythm of regularly sharing food and time together in the most practical, laid-back ways.

They were not practiced in the ways of formality or even basic planning ahead. There was no internet flooded with "recipes guaranteed to wow your guests."[i] No e-vites. No synced calendars. I suppose there was *Good Housekeeping* magazine, but I'm not sure what sort of leadership it provided in the '80s and '90s because we lacked the discretionary income for magazine subscriptions.

It all hung on the mustard-yellow rotary phone that might ring out at any moment from its post on the kitchen wall. We never knew who was on the other end until we answered it. When we were lucky, it was Betty or Deanne or my Aunt Maryann. "Want to head over? We're going to pop some corn." Or, "Have you eaten yet? I made too many beans."

I remember entire meals of corn on the cob in August followed by hand-cranked ice cream. There was the occasional

i. The first search result is a recipe for marinated feta, a high-brow accoutrement billed as a meal—which sort of sums up the bleak situation we find ourselves in.

pizza night and many bowls of chili. (Or as my parents call it, "chili soup." I don't know why.) Thinking back to those shared food experiences, I find the memory that lands with most clarity is the evening we gathered around our brown Formica kitchen counter to roll egg rolls and drop them into hot oil, a shockingly cultured experience for a bunch of small-town farm people.

Come + Eat

In the complex soup of wrangling meaningful community from the people near us, food shouldn't be what holds us back. If anything, it should be our greatest tool for togetherness.

The particulars are irrelevant. Not once have I walked away from someone's culinary offering disappointed or upset. Never have I thought less of someone because of the food they served. Have things gone awry? Of course! Kitchens are humbling spaces. Have there been times I didn't absolutely love the food? Perhaps, but it's honestly doubtful.[ii]

It's really not about the food. The food is just the vehicle that gets us to each other. We come together because we need evidence that we are not alone in this world or in our towns. We are not left to fend for ourselves.

Bri McKoy writes in *Come and Eat,*

ii. In this moment, I struggle to list foods I don't like or won't eat. The best I can do on the spot is beef liver, which I'm convinced no one under the age of sixty-eight enjoys. I also recall once making a complicated relish involving shaved fennel that reminded me of stale Easter candy.

The table breaks down the walls of social class and backgrounds and race. We are all one at the table, human beings receiving the necessary act of eating a meal. We are all citizens with one another. No other act of coming together so powerfully proclaims this.[1]

We're drawn to the idea of sitting across a table, face-to-face, because the hope of each other is reason enough to struggle through the honking horns and hotheads and dueling politicians each day seems to deliver.

The Hope + Healing of a Crunchy Taco Shell

We can continue to whisk complicated sauces and cook with hand-ground spices and anchovies—just maybe not when company comes over. In those moments, we can reach for the tried-and-true.

After all, most of us aren't foodies . . . we're hungry!

I submit the fastest, simplest way to build a relational storm shelter is the reckless deployment of taco night.

Listen closely. I'm not talking about authentic barbacoa cooked in an underground pit with ingredients that had to be sourced in advance. I'm not even talking about a taco bar with tableside guac. I'm surely not talking about wood-charred shrimp tacos with fire-roasted poblano purée or anything involving Manchego (unless those things happen to be your jam, in which case I will happily indulge you).

When I say taco night, I mean the version that is most accessible, requires the least amount of prep, and has very little overlap with actual tacos.

Surrounded by soybean fields, smack-dab in the middle of America, my family usually couldn't be bothered with taco shells. (When we did splurge on them, they came stacked in a box bought off the shelf at Kroger. One bite and the whole mess shattered into a pile on the paper plate.) Nope. Our "taco" riff (air quotes mandatory) consisted of crunched up Fritos topped with ground beef, lettuce, cheese, and, with any luck, a dollop of nonexpired sour cream. We inexplicably called this meal "straw hats," perhaps on account of the chip crumbs that formed a vaguely hat-shaped base, though we never set aside time to deconstruct this label.

One state away, in Indiana, my husband's family enjoyed a similar meal, subbing spaghetti meat sauce for the taco meat (an early red flag I'm glad I ignored) and naming them "hay stacks."

Straw? Hay?

This is what happens when Midwestern farm folks branch out for the sake of each other.

Now that we're in our current neighborhood, our taco night experience has leveled up considerably. The meal we're most consistently invited to share is, indeed, tacos. The real kind, with homemade, still-warm corn tortillas and a mixing bowl filled with diced onions. The kind that inspires emotion, undying devotion, and actual tears, depending on which salsa you drizzle on top.

No matter who we are, where we live, our budget, our station in life, our political or religious affiliations, the gray of our hair, the depth of the wrinkles between our brows (cough cough), or the level of lawlessness in our homes, taco night calls to us from the epicenter of humanity's Venn diagram, begging us to lay down our excuses and share a meal.

No Heroes at a Potluck

We know why it matters. We're as ready as we'll ever be to open the door and expose our homes and ourselves as utterly regular, caring only enough to wipe down the bathroom and shrug at the rest. We've established tacos as a suitable path forward.

But how exactly do we *do* this thing? How do we take it from "Fun idea!" to a sink full of dishes and a heart full of hope?

I'm not an expert but none of us is—or needs to be. Therein lies the beauty. Let's walk through it.

Step one: Establish the guest list. This already sounds way too highbrow, but all we're doing here is deciding who gets the call. Choose one person from your mental list of hopeful friends—or choose them all. It just depends on how much hamburger you have in the freezer.

Completing this shouldn't take more than three minutes. Go ahead and set a timer.

Here are two questions to guide your process. First, is there someone in a corner of your life you're drawn to? I can think of half a dozen people off the top of my head. These aren't complete strangers. I've had enough conversation with each of them to know I'd enjoy more. I know them. But I don't *know* them.

Second, can you think of someone who might be lonely? No one is immune to it. Some of my dearest friendships began when I recognized the loneliness in my heart reflected in someone else's eyes.

Inviting people into our homes is the surest, fastest way to span what divides us. So why am I already trying to talk myself out of it with an artful application of my go-to excuses? *I'm too busy; they're too busy; it sounds too hard.*

Hush up, unnecessary warning bells! These are ultra-low stakes. The task before us is simply to muster the courage to ask one little question. "Want to come for dinner Thursday night?" I recommend asking soon after the urge strikes, in an effort to sabotage any late-onset reservations. We need to back ourselves into a corner, because when it comes to putting ourselves out there, time is usually not our friend. The fear of rejection is real; it's one more reason we'd rather be invited than be the inviter.

Just remember, we are all living on the other side of someone else's anxieties. It always feels good to be asked and included. Put it out there. The worst they can say is no.

Step two: Send the text. I do miss the retro vibes of that rotary telephone, but a text is the most nonthreatening delivery, soothing the nerves of both sender and receiver alike.

Step three: Ask them to bring something. I've gotten better at sustaining a rhythm of inviting people in. But it takes work for me to ask them to contribute. This part is crucial, and it's a lesson I've learned (and relearned) the hard way.

We're good-hearted people. We like to make things easy for others. We don't want to burden anyone. The thing is, it's generally not a burden to grab a head of lettuce or a bag of cheese. When someone invites me to pitch in for a dinner at their home, I know it's going to be a fun, low-key evening, absent any complication.

One Necessary Caveat

One of my favorite food podcasts, *Black Girls Eating*, regularly discusses the politics, ethics, and equity of food. The word *politics* alone now triggers immediate reactions of party allegiance and divisive rhetoric, but in reality, politics encompasses the spectrum of government care for citizens—us and our neighbors. Michael Wear writes, "Politics is not important because we ascribe great value to political ideas, but because we ascribe great value to the human person."[2] From food deserts localized in both urban and rural communities, where access to healthy food is suppressed, to rampant food insecurity,[iii] to the villainizing of Southern soul food[iv] and certain international foods, the ways we think about, talk about, and form policy around economics and food have deep implications for our neighbors.

If we're sucking the marrow from the bones of true community, we will find ourselves sitting around a table

iii. Food insecurity is defined as "a lack of consistent access to enough food for everyone in the household to live an active, healthy life." In 2020, more than 38 million Americans experienced food insecurity, a number that increased to 42 million during the pandemic. See "Hunger in America," Feeding America, accessed January 25, 2022, https://www.feedingamerica.org/hunger-in-america.

iv. I recommend *High on the Hog*, a Netflix series that illuminates the roots of "Southern" soul food in the transatlantic slave trade.

with those who have more than us and those who have less.

It isn't ridiculous or dramatic to think a bag of cheese might cause real stress for someone. If we're living wide awake, we will be well-acquainted with the day-to-day struggles of far too many of the people around us.

There are absolutely circumstances that call for a "just show up" invitation, with the ultimate goal of honoring the dignity of our guests. It's good to thoughtfully discern our guests' needs while holding their dignity close in view. At times when I'm on the fence, my rule of thumb is that if they offer to bring something, I take them up on it.

What We Remember

If we can remember we all live as adjacent stitches in the same human quilt, then we can resist the urge to get too cerebral about the details. Keep it simple. Make it communal.

We don't have to let our limitations stop us. At times there might not be room in the budget to host a full meal so we turn to dessert or a glass of sweet tea. Maybe we don't feel like we have enough space to host a group so we pull lawn chairs into the yard or just vacuum the carpet and plop down on the floor. Most of us aren't afraid of doing things a bit outside the box. In fact, those are often the most memorable moments. As we move toward these easy rhythms of being together we'll find ourselves enjoying them more often.

Not long ago I got this text from my friend Alison:

> Good morning! I was thinking about chicken taco bowls for tonight? I have the chicken, sour cream, tomatoes, black olives, and some rice. I also have a bag of chips. What time are you free to come over?

I replied,

> I could make my famous rice.[v] Do you need any extra sour cream?

Voilà. It was the easiest thing in the world. I felt zero pressure to contribute but was thrilled to do so, since I was able. I didn't spend any extra money or make an extra trip to the store.

Simple is always the right answer.

Dinner that night was delicious, but what stuck with me most was everything else. Swaying on Alison's porch swing. The kids walking to the park to play kickball, followed by a town-wide game of bicycle hide-and-seek. The pop-up rain shower. Jon's terrible dad jokes. Driving home that night in a van full of tired kids and feeling contentment settle over me, that sleepy peace from being in the presence of people who know where all my skeletons are buried and love me anyway.

The taco bowls were simply the treasure map.

On Not Overthinking It

Our goal is to find a cadence of showing up and eating to-gether because we believe the table is a portal for connec-

---

v. Recipe for Shannan's famous rice: buy Mi Arroz seasoning mix in the little green box at Walmart. Add chopped onions and garlic if you're really feeling lavish.

tion. The rhythm can be as frequent as you'd like. If you're at a place where the preferred frequency is twice a year, no shame. To move from rarely throwing your front door open to committing to one repeatable annual effort is nothing to sneeze at.

We begin where we are. We get that first taste of belonging, disguised as each other. We find ourselves craving more.

Of course, it might seem easier to stick to our old routines. Why upset the dinnertime apple cart?

Some of us remember times we *did* put ourselves out there only to be rejected. It's tough to try again when our wounds haven't healed. I've been there, feeling like something must be fundamentally wrong with me. I've felt resentful for even trying. I've felt silly and overexposed. I know it's a gamble. For me, the moments that go right—the invitations that don't go unanswered, the evenings where I turn off the lights and fall into bed with a grin on my face— are those that help the bruises fade.

We long for easy, no-fuss friendships. They're worth the courage of trying again.

Carving out a new way requires some thought, some action, a little effort, and a moderate amount of grit. But we're ready to shake things up a bit. We aren't afraid to do the work. I know this because you're still with me, nearly halfway through this book.

If our choice is between ease or connection, we choose connection. We do so knowing the simplest plan wins. We can have that $5 deli cake and we can eat it too. With people we enjoy.

I've made my case for taco bowls, a tenet central to my worldview. But, though I struggle to even type these words, maybe you're not besotted by the inexplicable perfection that is meat, lettuce, and sour cream. (Always and forever, sour cream! Supreme me for life!) Maybe you just want a few more ideas. Perhaps, in my zeal, I've leaned too hard on taco night. (It wouldn't be the first time.)

It doesn't have to be tacos. Here are a few more time-tested ideas.

- Buy two of those enormous refrigerated pizzas from the grocery store deli and a large bag of knockoff Doritos. If you can't quite shake the urge to be extra, a bag of baby carrots and the bottle of ranch dressing floundering in your refrigerator door will carry you home.
- Lunchmeat sandwiches transform into something quasi-special if you serve them on buns and pop them under the broiler with a sprinkling of oregano.
- Take a page from my parents' 1980s playbook and bust out the vintage air popper to "pop some corn."

Opportunities to gather with the people around us are always well within reach—as long as we're looking for them.

Here's an example. On the heels of an intense summer of

racial reckoning, including within faith contexts, I decided to start a book club at church using Jemar Tisby's book *The Color of Compromise.* He writes, "The refusal to act in the midst of injustice is itself an act of injustice. Indifference to oppression perpetuates oppression."[3] A small but mighty group of us wanted to be part of meaningful action, to chip away at the stony response of much of the American church across history: to claim peace but preserve power. The conversation was overdue.

Hoping for as much engagement as possible, a careful calculation for a church as small and nontraditional as ours, I knew I had to keep it basic. I made the announcement without a lot of extra lead time. "We're doing this thing and it starts in two weeks. Right here. Right after church. Books will be provided free of charge.[vi] We'll serve a light lunch."

This light lunch equaled hot dogs, chips, and tap water in paper cups.

It worked so well that first week we kept the same menu for the duration of the study. Putting two teenage boys in charge of grilling upped the drama factor, but by week three, they had almost perfected cooking the interior of the dogs *and* the exterior.

As we sat together each week beneath the forgiving September sun, I was free to focus on the important discussion as it unfurled. Our shared hope for the future brought us

---

vi. Living in a low-income context has opened my eyes to the barriers we often build between ourselves and others. Requiring the purchase of a book can be a deal breaker for some. When possible, providing materials for everyone encourages participation and helps level out power imbalances.

together but a humble hot dog helped make it happen. To that, I raise my paper cup.

With Soup as Our Guide

After years of living here, I realized I knew *about* The Window, the local soup kitchen and food pantry, but I had never been inside and didn't *really* know the place. And so we bundled the kids up on the coldest day of that year and went for a grand tour: across cracked floor tiles, down dimly lit hallways, and through the receiving area stacked floor-to-ceiling with banana boxes filled with grocery store donations.

My brain went into problem-solving mode. I started asking questions. What do you need? (Everything.) What do you need most? (Take your pick.)

I noticed the rickety washer and dryer where clients could do their laundry. I thought of my bighearted online neighborhood and how easy it would be to crowdsource a new set. *Piece of cake.* I also imagined hosting a cereal or paper goods drive.[vii]

But I couldn't shake the kitchen—with its industrial ovens, three-bay sanitizing sinks, and skillets the size of compact cars. Lagging behind the rest of the group, I snapped a photo of the lone window overlooking a trash dumpster and parking lot. I'm still not sure why it grabbed me by the heart. But in the days that followed our tour, my

---

vii. Because basics like toilet paper, disposable diapers, and feminine hygiene products are not covered through government food assistance programs, these (expensive!) items are always in high demand.

mind kept drifting back to that orange-curtained window, that glass eye into a different world, one where people I love receive warmth and welcome, raising the temperature with their own good light. I stewed over it for weeks, then sent a smoke signal to the manager. "If you ever need help . . ."

Two months later I was officially Window staff, prepping and serving lunch for 120 people along with the rest of the crew. I spent hours chopping and stirring in a steamy kitchen—full days on my feet after years spent working at a computer. As it turns out, life was not asking for my concern, my good sense, or my fundraising abilities but rather for my actual embodied self.

Two days a week, I mix salads in bowls so massive the only pathway to completion is to use my (gloved) hands as shovels. I roll hundreds of turkey wraps, slathering each one with ranch dressing from an industrial-size tub. I de-eye potatoes for days and broil toast eight pans at a time.

One day we got a donation of fifty cases of oranges, and I sliced them until I lost circulation in my right thumb.

I still can't believe my luck.

I learn from my coworkers—hilarious, hardworking souls ranging from their twenties to their eighties who faithfully show up and throw their bodies against the work of ensuring everyone in our community has access to a hot, homemade lunch.

I learn from our clients, who arrive as their real selves, some bright, some surly, each of them holding the keys for our shared future. They ask for what they need, usually hot sauce (a need I share). They offer what they can. Some stay after lunch to stack chairs and wipe tables. Others help look after babies while mamas carry trays. I have learned some of their names and they've learned mine. Our dining room is living proof that eating together unites what the world tries to separate.

The food we serve—fresh, delicious meals made from castoffs and scraps—is a tribute to the art of collaboration. We are lunchtime evangelists in ironic T-shirts and grease-stained jeans, making magic with a whisk the length of my arm plus whatever donations happen to come in. A bit of fat,[viii] a tub of chopped onions, some broth, some veggies, maybe some meat. Once I was tasked with transforming leftover sloppy joe meat into "something vaguely Italian." Enter buckets of oregano! Tugboats of cheese! Voilà! Lunch is served.

Soup from stones. We dare you not to love it.

In a world foisting roasted meats, complicated chimi-churris, and yeasted breads upon the hospitality inclined, soup quietly waits to be noticed. We're looking for simplicity. For the opposite of complication.

Humble, sensible, and satisfying, may soup be our guide.

It's not about the food. It's about laughing, sharing, even disagreeing around the table. The food is just what gets us there.

Order pizza. Flip pancakes. Make casseroles cool again.

There's no wrong way, wrong menu, or wrong level of culinary skill. Find what works for you.

viii. I am the CBO—the Chief Bacon Officer—of the kitchen. We hoard our bacon grease like the liquified gold it is.

Tacos.
Soup.
Taco soup?
Let's eat.

Leftovers + Love

When I reflect on the most memorable meals I've eaten lately, there are several standouts.

The bowl of tomato soup in October, made on the fly by my friend Emily and eaten at her kitchen table while fat drops of North Carolina rain careened down the windowpanes. The spaghetti Cal offered to make one weeknight as I struggled to peel away from my work. The complicated three-layer chocolate caramel cream pie Ruby spent half the day baking for Thanksgiving. The plate of scrambled eggs and toast buttered to perfection by Cory, just last night.

The box of popsicles dropped off by Courtney when we all got strep throat. The bag of apples left on the porch by Dawn when the whole world went inside for a while. The watermelon Greg cut into thin, translucent slices just to show us the sophisticated Rorschach test blots hidden inside.

I remember Jodi standing in my kitchen with a grease-stained paper bag of warm apple fritters on a Saturday when I wasn't feeling well. And the night I spent on the other side of the country eating wood-fired pizza with brand-new friends. Halfway through the meal, Jonathon learned of our shared affection for PB&J and ceremoniously tore off a piece of flatbread, spread it with fig jam, and presented it to me like a pact.

There's no doubt these weren't the most sophisticated or complicated meals. They probably weren't even the most delicious, technically speaking. They weren't pricey, special occasion meals. In fact, I didn't pay a dime for a single bite.

These meals don't live tucked away in my memory because of their fussy ingredient list or elaborate presentation. I carry them with me because they arrived wrapped in belonging, fierce and undeniable. They transcended the culinary planes of delicious and nourishing and were so much more than food.

Each offering was a moment of recognition. An *I see you*. Every crumb carried the weight of kinship.

Food always tastes better when someone else makes it. This must be why. It turns out the sixth flavor profile is *intention*, and it trumps all the others.

We might be short on answers and solutions but we probably have some eggs and an onion, some bread, or a kettle already filled with water. Any one of those is a worthy starting point. This is the alchemy of leftovers and love.

It doesn't matter how comfortable or skilled we are in the kitchen. We don't have to be a foodie. (That might even get in the way.) The question we should be asking is not, Can I pull this off? but rather, Who needs to know they're not alone?

We aren't chefs or cooks. We're caretakers. Noticers. We

know how to feed people. We're at our best when we toss the complications and set our default to the basic act of sharing ourselves.

They say we eat first with our eyes, and maybe that's true. I would add that we eat forever with our tender, beating hearts. That's where the nourishment of kindness and care resides, keeping our hope above sea level.

This work requires all of us reaching out, taking turns.

Attention and intention. Eagerness to share. The full-throated belief that healing is always possible—and it often looks a lot like lunch.

This is our recipe for making it through.

ONE SIMPLE WAY
to Live as Neighbors

Make a pot of soup. In our attempts to create new, shared spaces of familiarity and comfort, soup is definitely our secret weapon.[ix]

Kendra Adachi, aka the Lazy Genius, tells us to "decide once" whenever possible, eliminating nonessential decisions from our routines. What if we officially decided that a double batch of soup is a worthy Sunday practice? Chili. Posole. Potato. Cheesy broccoli. Chicken and rice. Soup is endlessly adaptable and inexpensive. It easily accommodates a range of dietary needs and has cozy vibes for days.

ix. As much as I try to avoid war-related figures of speech, it has long been my dream to have T-shirts printed that say, "Make soup, not war!"

HEALING IS ALWAYS POSSIBLE— AND IT OFTEN LOOKS A LOT LIKE LUNCH.

Send that text today, before you have the chance to talk yourself out of it. Insist on keeping it simple. See how it revolutionizes your perspective. After all, *hospitality* is just a fancy word for "hanging out."

Maybe the following recipe will help.

Slow-Cooker White Chili

Because the only thing easier than regular soup is slow-cooker soup. Note: This "recipe" is a study on flexibility and preference, a very "to taste" and "based on availability" situation—which means you can't mess it up.

1 lb.(ish)	raw, boneless, skinless chicken (thighs or breasts)
1	onion, diced
2 (15 oz.) cans	white beans, drained and rinsed (black or pinto beans also work)
1 (15 oz.) can	corn, undrained
1 (10 oz.) can	diced tomatoes with chiles
1 cup	whatever random leftover salsa you have languishing in the fridge
2 tsp	cumin
1½ tsp	salt
1 tsp	pepper
1 tsp	garlic powder (or 2–3 chopped cloves of garlic)
1 tsp	chili powder
½ tsp	cayenne pepper (or sub with hot sauce, to taste)
1 (32 oz.) box	chicken broth (approx. 4 cups)
1 block (8 oz.)	cream cheese

Sauté onion in a small amount of oil to soften, then toss with all remaining ingredients except cream cheese into your slow cooker. Stir together and cook on low for 6 hours. Shred the chicken right in the cooker. Add the cream cheese and cook on high for at least another 20 minutes. Stir well before serving.

Top with tortilla chips, shredded cheese, diced avocado, cilantro, whatever you have on hand. I **highly** recommend adding a sprinkle of Tajín seasoning for an extra salty, limey, chili kick.

CHAPTER 6

Complexity > Comfort

> We embrace the abundance of community, leaning on each other through all life throws at us.

OUR FAMILY'S MOST CONSISTENT social gathering first formed a dozen years and two houses ago, back when Cal and Ruby were preschoolers and Silas was in Pull-Ups. We came together as near-strangers, people who shared no more than geographical proximity and the common discovery that our values and worldview no longer worked the way they used to.

In our case, these winds of change were primarily of a theological nature. Because we happen to be Jesusy people, we cobbled together this ragtag group for the sole purpose of eating homey casseroles and asking breezy questions such as, "Why *did* God give us free will?" and "What the heck, Job?"

After moving to Goshen a couple of years later, we started a new extension of this Monday night group, which morphed over time then morphed again. It seemed to exist in a near-constant state of change. New people arrived. Many lasted only a week or two—thanks, I'm sure, to our commitment to sarcasm, general brashness, and raging inability to progress through the book of Matthew at more than a glacial pace.

Our gathering looked different, in many ways, from its first iteration in our prior community. Here, the people were "new." Our meeting spot had jumped zip codes. Even the food that collected on the buffet table was notably different, due to Deb's prowess at deer hunting and Becca's refusal to cook anything, ever.[i]

What remained consistent was the meeting time, Monday nights at 7:00, and the collective sense that these evenings mattered. We circled many a theological drain but we circled them together.

The tie that bound us was not our charisma, our wisdom, our social proficiency, or our good looks. None of us fit precisely into the standard narrative of "nice church people." Our edges were jagged in places and we all had a tendency to ask questions we'd been taught we should keep to ourselves. We were arguers. Jokesters. Some weeks we accidentally skipped the Bible study altogether because Becca brought her mythical red accordion for show-and-tell

---

i. "I store the employee manuals from all of my previous jobs in my oven." —Becca

and most of us wanted to strap it to our chests and feel the heave.

We named ourselves The Misfits and grew to love one another deeply.

Time took its toll on us. Beloved friends relapsed, went back to jail, or lost custody of children whose birthdays we had lit candles for the previous year. Marriages crumbled beneath the weight of mental illness, poverty, or the blunt force of a world that roots against the success of some. We lost our wisest sage, the Misfit most likely to keep us on track through even the doldrums of Job, when he was moved to the graveyard shift at work.

We watched as Becca's health unraveled, her breath reducing to jagged rasps, the healthy glow dissolving from her cheeks. For a year, we relocated our gathering to a space where she could avoid stairs. On nights when she said she was coming but then didn't, we'd lock eyes with strained worry, tapping out safety-check text messages and only exhaling after someone's phone skidded across the table with a response. More than once, we visited her at the hospital, fearing the worst, only to have her bounce back and join us the following Monday as though she hadn't thumbed her nose at calamity. She didn't want to talk about it, so she made us laugh instead.

I was climbing the dunes near Lake Michigan with my kids when I got the call that Becca had died. The air was perfection and the sky was painted purple and persimmon. We still got ice cream cones as planned, but I cried into mine on the drive home, windows rolled all the way down, music playing too loud, my body fully alive to the reality that Becca was not. And I wasn't sure what we would do without her.

Jack was one of our quieter Misfits, but he and Becca shared an unspoken bond. She adored him. Truly *saw* him. A few days after she died, he showed up at our front door with a cash-stuffed envelope to put toward the plaque we planned to make in her memory.

Less than one year later, he messaged the group to say he'd been diagnosed with terminal cancer at age thirty-two. He wrote,

> One thought that quickly came to mind for me to cope was the thought of getting to see Becca and have a nice big laugh with her again.

The flowers we sent to his funeral were signed "With love, from The Misfits."

Week after week, regardless of what else was happening in the world or in the regular clutter of life, we sat knee-to-knee and looked each other in the eye. Together we created a parallel track of commitment and healing. We were known. We had people who held our quirks and tender stories with humor and care. We ate together, laughed together, and occasionally even cried together in our basement monastery made of faded carpet, burgundy chairs, and weeknight pasta bakes.

We thought the point was to study together and form some semblance of community. All the while, life lessons germinated undetected. What we really learned was that the greatest cost of love is pain.

Secondhand Smoke

Right now, as I write, November is having her way. The leaves flame crimson and gold, a million stained glass windows teaching us to hold on to the light we're given *and* to let go. Parker Palmer asks, "How shall we understand autumn's testimony that death and elegance go hand in hand?"[1] I say this is the trademark of most good things. Time is fleeting, we are frail, and living the good life together means we get it all, joy served up with heartbreak. "Community doesn't just create abundance," Palmer writes, "community *is* abundance."[2]

Late last night a friend sent a text saying someone she loved was in danger. I felt her pain across the miles. Today we woke to someone we love banging on our door, alone and terrified in the throes of a mental health crisis. A few hours later someone reached out just to tell me they loved me and they were praying for me. Being pressed against other people's battles and warming ourselves in their light means each day is a riot of emotion.

The complexity of community is the essence of community.

We are a caravan of travelers trudging in the same direction, weighed down with ideological baggage and marked by scars that don't seem to fade. It's messy or it isn't real. Our lives are on fire in a thousand different ways, no two burn patterns the same. In her sob-worthy song, "Come Close Now," Christa Wells finds poetry in the language of this pain, asking, "What can I bring to your fire?"[3] This is our reminder to expect the scent of smoke for as long as we're here.

It's not all tragedy. Lit by the embers of each other, we

remember we are not alone and carry that warmth with us. Building a future of togetherness is more than suffering and celebrating. It's about opening our hearts to what we find when we all haul our junk out into the same streets.

It might seem we have enough trouble and disappointment without borrowing more. But this is a catch-22 situation. Faithful companionship requires what it also provides: space for curiosity and room to grow. Just as the maple trees collapse into color so we become brighter with time, unafraid of the pain as we fall into each other.

Equip for the Expedition

As we set out to find our way to each other, our first step is to surrender to discomfort. It's not a threat. It's our guide. It means we're learning to be human, together, in broad daylight—honestly and with courage.

From there, we can put into practice a couple of underappreciated yet vitally important skills for the journey.

Become Ambassadors of Awkwardness

We are all a bunch of weirdos. I mean that in the very best way. We're inclined to think each embarrassing quirk and social faux pas is only ours, a thought that makes us want to burrow underground. But we are not alone. There is no such thing as "normal." My personal awkwardness inventory (easily distracted, hates small talk, prefers emotionally intrusive conversation, medium-bossy, would usually rather be reading) only highlights the fact that I am not what is commonly seen as someone naturally wired for community.

But I have a hunch most of us feel this way even though our details vary. So here we are, sharing a hunger for what's real even as we're repelled by situations in which we fear we won't measure up. It is truly a wonder we ever leave our homes.

There is no cure for this condition.

Awkward does not have to mean ill-equipped, or dysfunctional. It should not incite shame or inspire judgment. The feeling we tend to describe as "awkward" usually means *uncomfortable*, which is another way of saying *vulnerable* or *authentic*.

Awkwardness is fundamentally part of being human, and it's time to normalize it.[ii] It is not a puzzle that can be solved. If anything, it just needs a new PR campaign, and who better to launch it than us?

Do I have a second for this motion?

(Bangs gavel.)

Motion passed.

Stop Sidestepping Grief

I was at Kroger to get a last-minute ingredient for the weeknight dinnertime gauntlet. Rushed and frazzled, I hoped I could zoom in and out and get on with my life. I motored through the store with my foot on the gas, on-ramping to the pasta aisle—because we might not have it all together but we probably do have dried pasta and boiling water, and

---

ii. This logic, of course, also applies to the flagrant public wearing of socks with ankle-length jeans. IYKYK.

sometimes that feels like having it all. My narrow calculations for time and effort left no margin for the unexpected—yet when I came around the corner there they were, friends of ours who had recently suffered a quiet, painful loss.

My first impulse was avoidance, which says more about me than them. They are the sunniest of days, the bluest of skies, kindhearted and with the right amount of wit. But the clock was ticking and I did not know what to say in the face of their pain.

Social anxiety washed over me, my heart thumping, my cheeks heating, my mind racing. *What if they don't want to be reminded? What if they're having an okay day and by bringing it up I ruin it for them? What if they're also just trying to buy some marinara and get out of here?*

Presented with a split-second decision to meet them in their heartache, I opted instead for fake brightness, stupidly asking, "Hey! How are you guys doing?" as if I had no clue what they were going through or couldn't be bothered with the truth. I defaulted to the stalest crumbs of mindless pleasantry, forcing them to fumble through along with me before quickly parting ways.

My five-minute drive home was a full-strength shame spiral.

My knee-jerk choice of comfort over complexity lodged in my throat and tightened my jaw. I was tired of being afraid of someone else's suffering. I wanted to learn a better way.

At home, I went straight to my laptop and typed them a short apology, sincerely expressing what was buried beneath my own self-preservation. "I'm sorry for what you've been through and I regret I didn't say so in person. We love you and we're here for you."

It's hard to face someone else's pain. But with every honest attempt, we'll find ourselves closer to each other.

Uncovering Common Ground

On the heels of one of the most divisive US presidential elections in history,[iii] I detected the rattle of fear among people from all "sides" of the conversation. The specific worries were different, but it was a shared sense of dread and alarm that vibrated headlines, airwaves, and casual conversations. Captured by a strange tension in which those who had "won" and those who had "lost" were equally jittery, I embarked on a bite-size sociological survey via Instagram Stories.

My question: What are you afraid of?

I was unprepared for the sheer number of responses I received. At a time bankrupt of any collective unity, fear was our common ground. For hours I read, categorized, and tabulated each response into a squishy data set where "doing my best" was the extent of my scientific rigor.

The results were revealing. Topping the list by a long shot was the fear of *division*.

This four-alarm panic rang out from both sides of the political aisle as well as the middle. It didn't matter who we were, where we were from, or who we voted for. The future loomed apocalyptic, and we all believed we faced it alone.

---

iii. I tremble at the thought that this may, indeed, be a pattern that rages into the future.

Within the cohort of my DMs no one felt like a winner.

One woman wrote that she was afraid we won't be able to turn this around. She wasn't referring to a political party or those seated in power. She was talking about *us*. "Together" suddenly seemed broken. The chasm dividing us unnavigable. Our differences unscalable.

Looking toward a future shrouded in the fog of uncertainty and littered with broken relationships, we all seemed to be asking the same question. *Can we turn this around?*

Common ground isn't about agreement. It's about recognizing our shared humanity. Being willing to work for small slivers of mutual understanding is a mark of emotional maturity. It's not as elusive as we might think, if we're willing to wade in and listen to one another.

How willing are we?

I am convinced our path forward is paved in concrete and asphalt. It is the sidewalks, the back roads, the drive-thru lines, and the grocery aisles that will help us course-correct. Welcoming nuance with a soft heart and open arms is a skill on the decline. But we are up for the challenge because we refuse to believe that a healthier, kinder world is only a false hope or fantasy. We draw our water from the same source and load our children onto the same school buses. On my best days, I remember we want similar things. Peace. Liberation. Hope. Humor. Love. Companionship. Security.

I'm not trying to make light of the problem. More often than not, I'm worried about us too.

Truth remains true even when it's difficult and confusing. I am not at all certain we can fix this relational catastrophe. Common ground is not always possible or even advisable. There are times we will have to draw hard lines and grieve our losses. Still, reading the most vulnerable fears of those "on the other side" did something to me. I walked away not with a changed mind but with a softened heart.

Like it or not, we are shaped by our differences. Author and scholar Clint Smith writes that the complicated version of the story is the more accurate version.[4] Nearness sharpens our view of reality, which is why it can be a powerful agent of change.

To be positioned among different neighbors who hold different values and even fly different flags (why the politically branded flags, fellow Americans? Is this something we have the power to undo? Where did I put that gavel?) flusters and even angers me.[iv] The problem is these are people whose names I know. Our kids have played together. They are friends who have been kind to me. Who at times have dropped everything to help me.

Navigating differences with those closest to us might be the hardest work before us. I've heard countless stories of families shredding and churches splitting over political fallout. This is personal and painful for many of us. But the stakes are lower with the neighbor across the street. That makes him or her an ideal place to begin building our capacity for bearing tension as we work to see one another as fully, equally human.

This is our home and we all live here.

---

iv. Obnoxious political flags aside, there are some flags that should never be flown for any reason. If you'd like to read up on this topic, I recommend the book *How the Word Is Passed* by Clint Smith (New York: Little, Brown and Company, 2021).

The work is to keep finding ways to stick it out, moving toward each other as we go.

Two-Cake Monday

Tracy and her family arrived in our neighborhood and in our lives with the volume cranked all the way up. She was vibrant, funny, disarmingly kind. Watching her fling her full self into rebuilding after a lifetime of hardship was a master class in not taking a single thing for granted.

She walked across the street on Monday nights and took a seat with the rest of us Misfits as we tried to decode the mystery that kept us running together in the same direction—toward compassion, toward sacrifice, toward humility and honesty.

Tracy and her family made an abrupt departure well before the group died its own death during the winter of 2021, a convergence of COVID restrictions and the aftershocks of lives splintering off into different directions.

But before the layered grief of a good thing falling apart over time, we had so many moments when we saw, luminous and unobstructed, why it mattered to choose to belong to each other.

One of my favorite moments involved Tracy.

That night, like most Monday nights, I was scrambling for something to take to our potluck meal. Rummaging through the pantry, I found a box of cake mix and stirred together a random offering, hopeful that somewhere, a Misfit in another kitchen was preparing something that might pass as "nutritious."

A few minutes after I showed up with my cake, Maggie, another faithful Misfit, showed up with hers. It would be a two-cake Monday, a fortune no honest person has ever refused. We laughed it off as a funny coincidence. *Classic Misfits!* Then Tracy arrived. Barely through the door, one of her kids spotted the cakes and screamed, "Mom! They brought birthday cake for you!" Their wide-eyed astonishment was magnetic. We hadn't known it was her birthday, and yet there we were—with two flavor choices. Chocolate? Or white with sprinkles?

We raised our plastic forks to Tracy, to unexpected provision, to not being as in control as we pretend to be and seeing the value of dependence. With both Becca and Jack gone, our group had learned that sad days were never far away. But on that chilly winter night, we learned the next celebration wasn't either.

When life gives us two cakes, we eat them in good company, united by buttercream. Friendship doesn't have to be perfect or well-planned in order to be entirely delightful. It just has to be sincere.

John Green wrote, "We all know how loving ends. But I want to fall in love with the world anyway, to let it crack me open."[5] I'm with him. This is the delicious mess we've been given. Salty and sweet. Sunset-striped. So much more than *this* or *that*.

It's all coming for us.

We might as well be ready to love it.

ONE SIMPLE WAY
to Live as Neighbors

Like most important skills, learning to embrace complexity requires commitment. Lucky for us, daily life presents plenty of opportunity. Every crag and valley is a chance to practice sitting in discomfort, both our own and others'. When sadness, grief, anger, jealousy, or fear rises up, we can resist the urge to ignore it or distract ourselves from it. When someone holds their sorrows out with shaking hands, rather than offering anemic platitudes we can pull up a chair instead.

Maybe someone you know has suffered a loss and you either didn't know what to say or just let the moment pass you by, and you didn't say anything. Pull out a notecard and write them some heartfelt words. Drop it into the mail. It might feel too long overdue, but thoughtful nearness has no expiration date.

In the coming days, allow yourself to feel whatever you're feeling without judgment. We can't bright-side our way out of raw emotion. We don't have to scramble for solutions. Our emotions are neither bad nor good. They're truth-tellers and signposts.

When we downplay or ignore them, we're sure to end up lost.

When we sit close and suffer near, we find our way through.

CHAPTER 7

Tender > Tough

> We greet the world with our hearts exposed and
> our guards down.

I'VE NEVER CONSIDERED our corner of the neighborhood ripe for gossip, but a rumor recently swept through. Someone was building a fence.

The fact that this classified as buzzworthy should tell you everything about our snug little place. A week or so later I walked outside and there it was. It had gone up quickly, a tall stretch of solid plastic wall that ran the length of the owner's property line. Not a fence as much as a partition. Not a safety or privacy feature as much as an "I don't want to look at you" feature.

I cried a little, the day it went up.

I know what you might be thinking, because when I told this story to friends I've known for three decades, one of them gently said, with detectable confusion, "Shannan, people put up fences all the time."

This is true. Fences have no inherent moral value. Years ago, when Cal was tiny and braver than he should have been, we built our own fence in an attempt to protect him.[i] I get it.

But this neighborhood is different.

When we arrived, I didn't know our yard would extend all the way from the empty corner lot, with its lone apple tree, to Heather and Dustin's yard, where they would hang a sheet some summer nights and we'd watch *Boss Baby* while swatting at mosquitoes. It would blend seamlessly into Laura and Angel's yard, with the trampoline and the shared driveway perfect for riding scooters, and back to our "own" yard, with a playhouse and a tetherball pole. Four yards for the price of one.

An unsaid agreement was made somewhere along the line and it has worked well for us. Even after some neighbors moved away and new ones arrived, the pact stuck. Caleb plays whenever he wants on the backyard slide my kids now ignore. Viviana sends text messages saying things like, "Go on in. The door is unlocked!"

Yards aren't small when everyone shares.

Armor Off

How do we become more open, more trusting, more sensitive to the needs of others—especially within a culture that obsesses over *me* and *mine* and personal property/rights/

---

i. The day the fence was finished, complete with a complicated gate latch, Cal capped off his grand tour with a confident twist: "And this is how you get out!" He wasn't yet potty-trained and wouldn't master saying his *r*'s for several more years, but he cracked the latch code in less than one hour. Safety is a construct.

opinions? How do we work toward daring to unfence our actual selves?

When it comes to unguarding our hearts and increasing our social flexibilities, there's no recipe, DIY kit, or checklist. We can't buy our way to freedom or strong-arm ourselves into real-life belonging. We have to earn that emotional muscle mass by surrendering our ideas about things like independence, bootstraps, and general toughness.

Such defenses, rather than shielding us from some of the unnecessary traumas of being human, end up shielding us from being known.

There's nothing we need to add or apply. Here, it's all about stripping off protective layers and shedding our armor. After all, we aren't wedged into this cultural divide because we've been too kind or gracious toward each other. If we want admission into the club of the connected, then tenderness—living exposed to the relational elements—is the only required entry fee.

Our reward for working our way toward a thinner skin and allowing others in will be *each other*—along with a clear-eyed view of this fragile world. These are not small things. But odds are high that our popularity will suffer. Take heart. In becoming more tender to the tenderhearted, we will also discover inner fortitude against the mean and narrow-minded.

It's not thicker skin we need. It's a commitment to tenderness.

IT'S NOT THICKER SKIN WE NEED. IT'S A COMMITMENT TO TENDERNESS.

Reconsidering "Capable"

First, we disabuse ourselves of our hidden (and not so hidden) hero complexes. All our lives we're patted on the head, lauded, promoted, and admired for our ability to effectively multitask. We're called self-starters, as though going it alone is somehow better than working together. We generate results. We do the things and we do them well.

Many moons ago, one of my bosses chose me for an important project because "the building could be burning down and Shannan wouldn't show a flicker of alarm." Pals, this is not an admirable trait. This is emotional dysfunction, the fruit of a society that rewards the ones who do not run screaming from burning buildings. At that time, I was in the unhealthiest season of my life, but I had learned to bury my needs, cover my scars, and swallow my questions. My active dissociation from myself was rewarded with a promotion—and on and on it goes.

I'm not saying we can't thrive at everyday living. We just need to be cautious about what we admire and reward, in ourselves and for others. Everyone needs help sometimes. Let's destigmatize this in a hurry.

Redefining "Strong"

Perhaps because I grew up a gangly, puny-looking child, I've spent most of my life overcompensating, hell-bent on proving my strength in other ways. I downplay routine illnesses. I lean into conflict when others retreat. It's not out of the question for me to lead sporadic online revolutions. Even my physiology is on board, quietly signing the team pledge to avoid crying in public at all costs. All for the sake of appearing tough. When one of my kids lamented a friend who "cries all the time! Like, once a week!" I knew there was trouble and that the call was coming from inside the house, so to speak. It was a gut-punch to see the ways my unhealthy emotional defenses had projected onto them. I don't want them to believe normal emotions or showing weakness are "bad." I don't want that for myself either.

I'm on a personal mission to become more emotionally honest and healthy. There are no awards for bottling up sadness or trophies for hiding weakness. Our culture might value rugged brawn and stone-faced composure, but we see where that got us. We all have our go-to "strength" armor. I'm proposing we go ahead and remove it, and I'm suggesting we're actually more "us" without it.

Re-examining "Wealthy"

Oy, the money one. The mere fact that we're all scrambling for the psychological "Exit" sign is proof we need this on the list. I come to you as someone who for most of the last decade lived paycheck to paycheck. Our kids received government health insurance. Prior to a year ago, we had two geriatric vehicles with no A/C.

I'm not trying to wage a perverse Financial Hunger Games by listing these examples. I just think it's time to build some cultural stamina for financial transparency. These Martin financial histories are true.

But these realities are also true: we are a family with two vehicles. To my great embarrassment, neither lives in our garage because it's packed with so much other *stuff*. (Let that sink in.) We eat at restaurants, take vacations, and buy too many books. The pile of shoes inside our door tells its own testimony.

Compared to the rest of the developed world, America has one of the highest levels of economic inequality, which means the division between the rich and the poor is widest.[1] Among its nine most closely related international "peers," it ranks highest. Practically speaking, a deep economic divide exists in what is considered a wealth-saturated country.

Financial status is primarily a function of perspective. Regardless of where we live, most of us are geographically near both the affluent and those living in poverty. It's all too easy for me to feel put-upon that I have to drive with the windows down, sweating bullets, in August. But viewed from the perspective of abundance over scarcity, many of my neighbors don't own a vehicle at all.

Most of us reading this are statistically among the richest people in the world.[2] If this doesn't feel true to us, it might be because we tend to measure ourselves against those who have more than us, not less.

This isn't a call to immediately liquify all assets as much as a plea for honest assessment. If we can look these facts full in the face, maybe we can also begin to choose differently. We can give more generously. We can adjust our relationship with capitalism-run-amok, deferring to a position of "enough" rather than climbing and acquiring and believing we need the newer, better version of [NAME YOUR POISON] every time one comes along. We can view our wealth as a hurdle to overcome or as a resource for the flourishing of others rather than a marker of personal success.

Rethinking "Independent"

All of the above boils down to the prized societal virtue of independence, which can be defined as "the absence of need." We seek a way of life where we lack nothing, yet to do so is to end up missing out on the easy solace of community.

A man in Ecuador once told me a story about an indigenous tribe in the Amazon rainforest. From the outside, they seemed deeply in need of some modern necessities, so a group came together to provide them with electricity, believing it would improve their lifestyle. It wasn't long before the tribe rejected it, saying, "No one was coming to the center of the village anymore, to sit around the fire together."

If we allow ourselves to move through this world capable, strong, and wealthy, never needing anything from those around us, perfectly proud of our ability to take care of ourselves, it will be to the detriment of our truest, tenderest beating hearts, whose longing for closeness with others requires constant protection.

The Power of Names

Back when our kids were still in elementary school, our public school system took up the long-overdue cause of rebranding its mascot from "Redsk*ns"[ii] to "Redhawks."

ii. This term is widely regarded as pejorative. *Merriam-Webster* dictionary lists it as "offensive" and "insulting." See https://www.merriam-webster.com/dictionary/redskin.

The public conversation plays in my memory almost as if it was a television show I'd watched. In a testament to how our place changes us over time, I was not part of the debate, a fact I can scarcely fathom today. I absorbed it from the periphery, taking in only its broad themes.

At the time, my understanding of such matters was shallow. The public school I'd attended had a variation of the same offensive mascot and did little to educate me about the deep, pain-ridden history of our nation's founding. What I'd learned was largely theoretical and far from personal—an ancient, dishonestly told history. Now I had friends and acquaintances on both sides of the argument. I was invested and listening. It wasn't long before I realized I was siding with those in favor of the change.

As stated in Goshen College's land acknowledgment:[iii]

> We want to acknowledge that we gather [on] the traditional land of the Potawatomi and Miami Peoples past and present, and honor with gratitude the land itself and the people who have stewarded it throughout the generations. This calls us to commit to continuing to learn how to be better stewards of the land we inhabit as well.[3]

To be a good neighbor is to tell the truth and work toward repair.

---

iii. This idea of acknowledging the history and original ownership of the land was foreign to me a few years ago. Though this can be a meaningful way of honoring Indigenous peoples, it can also become a performative act if not coupled with intentional reeducation and a consistent pursuit of justice.

Thinning Our Skin

In her book *The Liturgy of Politics*, Kaitlyn Schiess writes, "The strongest forces in our lives are . . . the bodily rituals we participate in, the stories we tell and live into, and the communities that give us belonging and meaning."[4] After a lifetime of hearing that people were becoming "too sensitive" or "too PC" (politically correct), and that thicker skin was in order, I now lived in a place where my beliefs were hurting people near me.

Though it took time for me to see it, my neighbors were reshaping the ways I saw the world and my place in it. My brittle allegiance to a "suck it up" toughness was giving way to a new sort of softness. I realized if I could only be resolute about one thing, I wanted it to be kindness—particularly toward those at the short end of power. I wanted to be someone who actively tried to avoid causing pain, even if I still had a lot to learn about the ins and outs of cultural and interpersonal dynamics.

After months of contentious Facebook posts and "Save Our Mascot" efforts, the change was made by our school board by a vote of 5–2. Rereading the history of this event, I can see it was mostly BIPOC[iv] people saying, "This is harmful. This hurts people." Conversely, it was primarily White people saying, "What's the big deal? It's fine!"

Clint Smith defines history as what we need to know and nostalgia as what we want to hear.[5] When it came to an issue that was deeply, painfully personal to our community,

---

iv. Black, Indigenous, People of Color (some find this more inclusive than "people of color").

many White residents were unable or unwilling to listen, all for the sake of nostalgia. The decision was a victory, albeit one layered with trauma for many.

When we discover that something we say has hurt someone, we can choose to be "too sensitive" on their behalf, immediately course-correcting—even if, as journalist Hanif Abdurraqib might say, we have "different eyes on the world."[6] Setting our default to the comfort and safety of the marginalized is an act of heartfelt generosity.

But I Can't Keep Up!

Our language, our word choices, and the names we ascribe matter deeply. I know this is a fast-moving target. For example, Cory and I have been talking lately about shifting our language from the customary label of "inmate" to "incarcerated person," or even better, "person who is incarcerated." You might rightly discern that this shift takes us from two syllables to nine, so I suppose the case could be made that the update is more difficult in the technical sense. You might also have the urge to rattle off people you know who are or have been incarcerated, and being labeled as an inmate "doesn't bother them at all!" Maybe even *they* think this move toward person-first language is a bunch of bunk.

What I am suggesting is that regardless of every personal anecdote the world over, it is not only easier to make the change toward more humanizing, person-first language but also never wrong to lean in toward each other in thoughtful solidarity.

Of course, we could also choose to throw our hands up and proclaim defeat, retreating to, "This is impossible! I can't keep up! People need a thicker skin!"

This dismissive stance might stem from the sincere fear of getting something wrong. While this might be a thoughtful concern, it can also be the very thing that holds us back from being an active participant in the work of wholeness. As Cole Arthur Riley writes, "Liberation is for those who tremble."[7] We must be willing to enter into these delicate spaces and conversations as learners.

There will be times we have to do it scared.

Dominant culture comes with the built-in advantage to choose our own comfort over the dignity of others. Often this default mode is not something we even see. It is simply the air we breathe. As we widen our circles there will be moments when we realize our bandwidth for bearing these tensions is low. Rather than being overwhelmed by the ever-changing "rules" of language and power of naming, we could receive it as an opportunity to embody the grit of tenderness and nurture a healthier, more inclusive community.

It *is* a lot to keep up with, but what an honor to keep trying.

Disagreeing Well

As we move out of our personal comfort zones and toward one another, disagreements should be expected in that practical, shoulder-shrug "of course" sort of way. This doesn't have to be a big deal, especially if we proceed with a plan, because not all disagreements need to unravel into full-blown arguments.

Living with each other at the forefront of our minds means inviting vulnerability and friction. Both are wonderful teachers but only if we're willing to stay in the classroom. That's the first step in navigating minor squabbles: *stay put.* Most of us do not relish conflict and will do almost anything to avoid it. As someone with a larger bandwidth for this, even I would often rather fly away than stay and fight. But it is only in working *through* the problem that we untangle it.

At the advice of my husband, teenagers, close friends, and parents, I'll keep my words on this topic few, as I am still very much a work in progress. Here's what I do know, thanks largely to the patient people around me.

First, don't enter disagreements uninformed. As my dad reminded us over the years, "Even a fool looks wise when he keeps his mouth shut."[v] While we shouldn't feel we have to be an expert on every topic or command all of the research, if we aren't at least minimally versed on the topic at hand, we are not invited to the stress rally.

Second, resist defensiveness. Defensiveness is our signal that we're making something personal when it's often not. It's what happens when we let our unresolved junk obstruct our ability to listen objectively and see clearly. Sooner or later, we'll all stare this one down. Rather than allowing it to take over, let's heed the alarm to refocus our attention away from ourselves, choosing common ground over self-protection.

v. Proverbs 17:28.

And third, stay humble. Find yourself at the wrong end of someone's bad day? Stay humble. We've all been there. Riled up because you know you're right? Stay humble. They probably feel the same way. Wanting to unleash a torrent of angry witticisms and timely truths because you're sick and tired of the resounding injustice and pervasive selfishness of humanity?[vi] Stay humble. We can't tyrannize our way to harmony. (I've tried.)

Maybe a few simple ground rules will help. I hereby propose these core values:

We will use humanizing language at all times.

We will honor the *imago Dei*[vii] and full dignity of everyone.

We will value the cognitive pain of critical thinking.

We will seek the emotional discomfort of leaving our silos in order to embrace a diversity of experience and opinion.

We will boldly stand for justice, employing boundaries when necessary while doing our best to remember the humanity of those who oppose us.

Holding Space for What's True

In the summer of 2020, I was invited to be part of an intensive ten-hour "race circle" with five White participants

vi. Maybe it's just me?

vii. *Imago Dei* is Latin for "made in God's image," a tenet central to Christian belief.

and six Black participants. The group represented an array of life experiences and spanned perspectives informed by gender, socioeconomic status, education, upbringing, politics, and religion.

Each participant received an equal amount of time to speak, which meant we all listened far more than we talked.

At our last session, the facilitator asked us to think of an instance when we were the ethnic or "racial" minority, with the caveat that we were not allowed to list international travel as our example.

As one of the Black participants articulated, "I grew up in a White world. I know a lot about it."

For us White participants, the question was sobering. Some of us had to admit we had never experienced being the minority. At first, I thought of many experiences at my kids' former elementary school, where the vast majority of families were Latine. But the more I considered those moments, it was obvious that while the numbers had been "against" me in those situations, due to the fact that the majority of teachers, administrators, and even parent leaders were also White, I still sat on the side of "power."

These are unsettling things to talk about.

The recent common narrative has shifted hard toward these conversations around race and privilege being damaging to White people. Some would say that to acknowledge the systems we are part of as problematic is to cause irreparable harm to ourselves (or our kids).

This isn't so. It will not emotionally destroy us to learn the full, true history of where we arrived from and what it all means. We are resilient hope-holders. If we want to walk toward healing, there's a lot we need to learn.

In her chapter titled "Your Name Is Not Racist, It's Beloved," Black author, pastor, and podcaster Osheta Moore writes, "When you are grounded in something other than your works or results, when you are grounded in a truer, deeper, soul-healing confidence, you can continue to press on—even if it means death to all your comforts and control." She continues, "White Peacemaker, own your Belovedness so that you can proclaim mine."[8]

There is no shame in bearing witness to what is true. There is no shame in sitting in the tension. There is no shame in admitting that our experiences are different and we recognize the problems at hand.

Acknowledgment is its own beginning.

The Circles We Don't See

Being part of the race circle was a hopeful learning exercise for me. I took pages of notes and walked away more optimistic about the future of togetherness than I had previously been.

It didn't take long for life to kick my optimism in the knees.

I was sitting in a public space, surrounded by other White people, when a group of strangers began conversing about their views on race, policing, and who deserved what. Their words were beyond disheartening, but even more, I couldn't escape the fact that they felt safe to speak their opinions in my presence simply because I shared their skin tone. They seemed neither uncomfortable nor even cautious about trading nakedly racist viewpoints in my midst.

If I had to guess, I would imagine they dwelled in an echo chamber, without meaningful closeness with people who don't reflect themselves.

Tenderness requires friction. We have to be willing to bump against new ideas and feel the shrapnel of toxic histories. We have to come close in order for the best of us to rub off on each other.

If we're willing to lay our hearts bare, life becomes a series of astonishments as we carry each other through it all.

Isn't that the dream?

Finding the Light

The morning after a presidential election of enormous consequence, I read the social media post of one of my neighbors: "I am a Dreamer. We are very afraid." We'd lived here for many years, solidly anchored to our new community with the thinner skin to prove it, but there was still so much I did not know. Those eight words began my crash course in understanding that democracy means different things to different people.

My neighbors never asked who I voted for. They weren't interested in waging political skirmishes.

We all just want to know we are loved and that we're not alone. When hard days come, we need to feel some of our grief seep into someone else's bones.

The intervening days after that election were a collision of worldviews. Some people in my life were celebrating. Others were terrified about their futures. The dissonance was deafening.

Two days after it was all said and done, a young neighbor showed up at our front door holding a plastic juice pitcher of posole verde. Amid uncertainty and, for many, actual fear, his family chose to reach out in tender solidarity, delivering comfort to the ones who needed it the least.

Times are tough but we don't have to be. The war we're in is not the war we *think* we're in. Our fight is against the darkness of self-protection and the fear of getting too close.

I used to think of the word *independence* as a synonym for *freedom*. Now I see them as opposites. To live as a neighbor is to reside in the location of someone else, *with* them, and to try to see the world from their vantage point. It is to draw near in mercy. To defer. To live by the Platinum Rule (an upgrade from the Golden Rule), in which we treat others as *they* wish to be treated.[9]

Safe distance is never really safe. We do not grow kinder in empty rooms. Which will we choose? Fences or soup? Me or us?

Here, in the fragile threads that knit us together—our intertwining histories, differences, quirks, strengths, and secret recipes—we recognize our safety in numbers and the security we crave.

So, we build patio decks, not fences. Stir soup instead of disdain.

We let our hearts be split wide open, receiving tenderness as our birthright, and the light spills in.

ONE SIMPLE WAY
to Live as Neighbors

As we work toward the safety and needs of others, it's vital we reexamine our long-held beliefs, especially those we inherited or absorbed from majority culture without the benefit of personal critical thought.

When we discover our beliefs being challenged in some way, rather than landing on defensiveness or pushing the thought away, it might be more productive to guide ourselves through the cognitive struggle with these simple questions:

Is this true?

Who is it true for?

Who might it leave behind?

How is this belief forming me?

Is it making me softer? More open? More aware?

Is it building walls between me and others?

Is it reinforcing my own sense of comfort?

Is it making me a truer reflection of the person I want to be?

Taking the time to reconsider things we haven't adequately

interrogated is worthy inner work. It's time for us to reclaim "too sensitive" as our honor badge for everyday citizenship. Pin it on. Let's carry these questions into our shared future, on the lookout for who we might be missing.

In the end, it is only our tender attention to one another that will make the world safer, brighter, truer.

CHAPTER 8

Practice > Preach

> We believe embodied, intentional action is the glue of healthy communities.

I WAS SITTING ALONE AT THE ELECTRIC BREW, working on a writing project, when my cell phone rang. On the other line was my then-thirteen-year-old son, Cal, who was riding his bike to a summer orchestra rehearsal. "Mom, a truck hit me. I think I'm okay. But can you come?"

My body has not forgotten that moment.

Though the rational portion of my brain computed that he was safe and well enough to make the call (and my general tendency is to remain oddly calm in crisis[i]), my lizard brain was racing around my skull, banging pots and pans. *THIS IS BAD!* Calm is a reliable mask for fear, but it generally does us no favors. I was scared to death.

I stood up, half-frozen yet frantic, my table covered

---

i. Unless there's blood. In which case, NOT CALM.

with my open laptop, multiple books, and pages of notes. A stranger who had overheard my side of the call waved me toward the door. "Just go."

I left everything behind, jumped in my van, and followed the sound of sirens.

At the scene, a police officer stopped traffic to help clear my path to my child, who was at the center of a tangle of emergency responders. His bike was damaged beyond repair, as were his eyeglasses and his violin. But he walked away with just a bit of road rash and a few scrapes. A woman standing next to him met my eyes and said, "I saw it happen. I waited here with him, as a mom, until you could come."

That evening, I published the obligatory social media post.

By the next day, Instagram had done its work. The surrogate crisis-mom who mothered my child for those agonizing minutes with tears in her own eyes was a woman named Leah.

I reached out to thank her. We've been friends ever since.

Reaching for Each Other

Though I never want to relive that crisis, the way it unfolded is the actual dream we hold.

At every harrowing turn, people built bridges over our troubled waters with their actual selves. Even the guy who hit Cal did the right thing. He called for help. He stayed.

If we long for a reality where we are held and cared for in our scariest moments, we have to be willing to step into the fray for those around *us.*

We have to be the neighbor/friend/impromptu mother we will inevitably need.

We have to be willing to go first. In this context the directive sounds a bit simplistic and even unnecessary. Have we stooped so low as a society that we have to plead with one another to pull over and help a child struck by a pickup truck?

No, I don't think so.

Leah did what most of us would instinctively do: cut through the caution tape and enter in. We would offer a cool hand of comfort, a steadying presence, the vigilance and nurture that hold us all together. Of course we would.

Sebastian Junger writes, "Humans are so strongly wired to help one another—and enjoy such enormous social benefits from doing so—that people regularly risk their lives for complete strangers."[1]

Even when the stakes are highest—when life and death are on the line—we are programmed to act. It's a relief to know we have someone in our corner in the very worst of times.

The real question is, What will we do the other 99 percent of the time? What sorts of situations warrant our involvement? Who deserves our risk? How far are we willing to take this idea of acting on behalf of others? How close is close enough?

More Than Words

In June 2020, I woke up to find my Instagram feed stacked with empty black squares. What I initially thought was a bug in the system was actually a flash movement initiated by Black musicians and artists in protest of George Floyd's murder.

In no time, their strategy jumped from the music industry to social media, where White women waiting for a way to prove they cared seized upon it with a vengeance: #blackouttuesday was everywhere.

At that time, I was finding my rhythm and owning my voice while in many ways my life and even my activism were marked by the ease of my social location. As a White woman, speaking out was something I could choose to pick up and put down. It was not a daily lived experience for me as it was for people of color. I had to reckon with the dual nature of coming alongside those fighting for their very lives while simultaneously understanding that my fringe involvement in the cause would never carry the same risks. My experience did not have the same urgency or gravity. But that wasn't an excuse to sit it out either.

Beneath the storm clouds of a global pandemic and the end of normalcy as we knew it, Ahmaud Arbery was killed. Then Breonna Taylor. Then George Floyd. As disappointing as it was, it seemed many White people required these compounding traumas in order to snap awake to the problem. For the first time, my family painted signs and joined a peaceful protest at the local courthouse, standing with our neighbors to call for attention, oversight, different policies, a better way. Later that night, one of my kids said, "I could feel their pain. I understand."[ii] Peace can be intense sometimes.

ii. My kiddo has been on the receiving end of racism, as have all of my kids. It was important for me to see and enter into their pain, but I will never understand it in the same way they do.

Though our contribution was important, in light of the national conversation and its mounting tensions it still felt minuscule.

When #blackouttuesday arrived, my first impulse was to post a black square of my own. However, after reading the words of some of my Black friends and doing my own research, complications emerged. There was a real fear that the good intentions behind those black squares might inadvertently suppress vital information or even slow the momentum of those who were crying out for justice in ways that were riskier and far more personal than a single social media post.

Even so, after weighing the opposing "sides" of this brand-new digital clash, I blacked out my screen, doing my best to use the correct and most helpful hashtags. The likes and comments flooded in. It felt good to be part of something larger than myself and stand with those committed to protecting Black lives.

When oppression reveals itself, it can be simultaneously soothing and empowering to join the chorus against it. Especially when it's as easy as posting a black square on Instagram.

In the months that followed, a new narrative emerged among my BIPOC friends. It went something like this:

We saw your black squares, but where are you now? What are you actually doing about it? Have you forgotten? Why did you already unfollow us? Did you read one book and call it a day? Do you really care? Because you've gotten real quiet, and we notice. If your black box wasn't partnered with meaningful action, it was nothing more than a show.[iii]

The internet is a powerful tool for imagining a better future. It illuminates injustice and streamlines the resistance. It also makes it all too easy to confuse preaching with practice.

Words that rattle around in our heads but fail to actually move us toward lower, grittier, more local places are nothing more than ear candy. A fizzy pop jingle that lodges itself in our psyche but holds no real significance.

Cheap words that make us look good are the essence of performance. We can't holler our way toward a safer future.

Strong communities are not built from hot takes. They require action—the back-aching, heart-splitting, hand-callousing, funky-sweating embodied presence that proves we're in this thing together.

Where Do I Start?

Here's the tricky thing: no one is expected to enter into every conflict. We are finite people with only so many hours in a day. Right now, and just generally speaking, I'm staring down a sink full of dirty dishes, a pile of back-to-school forms, an intense work deadline, a stack of overdue library books, and a minivan that will hopefully make it to the gas station on fumes. The gunk clogging your drain might look different but we've all got some.

iii. An amalgamation of responses from many of my friends and favorite Instagram accounts.

Life is already too much *and* not enough. And now we're supposed to involve ourselves in other people's problems?

Yes. We are. Not out of sheer obligation or performative duty and not because we're equipped to save anyone from anything but because, counterintuitively, holding on to each other through dark nights and bewildering days is the key to our shared liberation—the kind where no one is left behind. In struggling forward with each other we remember we are not alone.

Where do we begin? We begin where our feet are standing. We begin where our hearts pound in our chests or our righteous anger swells. We begin with the seemingly small thing that dissolves our self-sufficiency into salty tears.

What do we see?

What makes us feel?

What keeps us up at night?

That's where we begin.

Mind the Gap

Often, it's a specific issue that lassoes our hearts. We hear about something in the news or read a post on social media and a light bulb begins glowing in a corner of ourselves we didn't even know was dark.

We should stay alert to causes that ignite our hearts and bodies. But if we want to be on the team rather than just a spectator, it's important to locate the bridges between issues and living, breathing people. We might walk toward a cause but we'll stick around and get our hands dirty for the friendship.

Here's an example.

Twelve years ago, when I lived in the country and called myself Flower Patch Farmgirl[iv] on the internet, I received an email from a publicist asking if I would like a copy of the forthcoming book *Tattoos on the Heart* by Gregory Boyle.

The idea that someone would send me a free book in the mail was all the luck and good fortune I could imagine. The nerdiest windfall!

At that time, I didn't know anyone who had been incarcerated or gang-affiliated. I didn't have a relationship with a single Latine person. Not to mention I had never met a Jesuit priest. And the road trip to Los Angeles my family had taken when I was in middle school probably didn't equip me with all the nuances of the city. On its face, I was far outside the Venn diagram of Boyle's writing.

But I *was* in the first phase of waking up to injustice and becoming more thoughtful about people who did not look, live, or believe exactly as I did. That free mystery book swept me into the unfamiliar sea of people caught in the criminal legal system.[v] By chapter 2, my paradigm was shifting.

Soon after, we met a man who lived in a tent encampment (another experience I had never contemplated). When he wound up in jail on petty charges we sent letters, and when he was released Cory picked him up and brought him over for a dinner of hot dogs and mac and cheese. After I apologized for the meager offering, he said, "What more could I

iv. Bless. Bless my adorable heart. Bless my readers. Bless us, Lord.

v. I can no longer, in good conscience, refer to it as the "criminal justice system."

ask for? This is classic comfort food!" (This might have been the start of my crash course in aiming for familiar > fussy.)

From there, the maddening world of incarceration and reentry unfolded before us. Most notably, Robert (not yet officially part of our family at the time) was incarcerated. Visiting with him from the janky phones in the lobby was our first exposure to a jail. Eventually, Cory made the unexpected transition into his current work as the chaplain for the same jail.

These days, many of the people in our lives have been detained by this system. Our nearness to them, witness to their talents, attentiveness to their needs, and belief in their experiences fuel us to work for the repair of an institution that preaches healing but inflicts further trauma. I'll be forever grateful for that book, but without me bridging its instruction to actual people in my direct line of vision (whether I realized they were there or not), my fledgling interest would not have found the will to persist.

It's easier to defend a cause than it is to show up and walk with real people through the low tides of life. We might feel good when we define ourselves by our own beliefs and smart opinions, but lacing up our boots for the sake of a suffering brother or sister complicates things.

Once we've witnessed the hardships of someone we care about, it's harder to cast judgment. Things become personal. We're placed on the same patch of earth, which changes everything. This summation of Father Gustavo Gutiérrez's message cuts straight to the heart of it: "So, you say you love the poor? Then name them."[2]

I'm no longer inclined to label anyone "poor" because we're all carting around our own particular poverties. There's no us/them, rich/poor, or needy/generous. There is only us. "Love exists only among equals."[3]

We can't claim to love what we don't know.

We can't know what we don't see.

We can't fully *see* anything if we don't put our bodies in places of tension and pain.

There's a massive difference between loving people in theory and loving them in the moment—by name. It's up to us to choose. Are we content to stand on a digital street corner and preach? Or are we ready to throw down our megaphones and walk straight into traffic?

> We can support thoughtful, robust, hospitable immigration policy *by walking* with a newcomer.
>
> We can care about incarceration reform *by befriending* a formerly incarcerated person as they reenter and rebuild.
>
> We can value life *by welcoming* a single parent and their child/children into the regular rhythm of our days, providing backup through the struggle, and celebrating their wins.

The possibilities are endless.

Ask for What You Need + Offer What You Can

One winter I was invited to join a group of local citizens and leaders committed to the health of our underresourced and overlooked neighborhood. The group operated from an ABCD framework—Asset-Based Community Development—that views community engagement through the lens of existing strengths rather than deficits.[4] *What treasures do the community and its citizens already hold?*

We met in an upper room of a historic house-turned-public-health-facility and circled up in folding chairs on the worn wood floor. Each meeting began with the question, How are you arriving? and ended with, How are you leaving? This short, grounding exercise built trust between us. It also lent important perspective, reminding us first that we are small but significant parts of the whole.

We're not saviors, philosophers, monarchs, or social scientists, just regular neighbors doing our best with what we've got, sometimes failing, and often feeling overwhelmed.

At our second meeting, I noticed an unassuming sign taped to the wall. "Ask for what you need. Offer what you can." My eyes kept drifting toward it, then to the towering pines outside the windows, then to the neighborhood beyond, and finally to the snow-dusted peak of my own roofline, perfectly visible from our bird's-eye view. Concentric circles of belonging.

I instantly adopted that mantra as a basic instruction for life.

It's both simple and profound, a two-way street, with no overpasses or detours. The sign didn't say, "Ask for what you need. Give all you have and fix every problem immediately." There's no pressure or power imbalance, no good reason to grind ourselves into dust whenever a need arises, which is constantly.

This is our lantern in the night as we push ahead toward necessary change.

Unfussy Bonds

The elementary school at the end of our street long ago invaded my heart and set up camp there. With our three youngest kids now well into their teen years, walking to its doors each morning is one of my favorite memories.

In her book *Learning in Public*, Courtney E. Martin shares her family's experience in a global-majority, low-income public elementary school in Oakland, California.[5] She writes honestly about the complexities of school integration, why so many White parents opt out of the system, and the tendency toward harm among those who stay, including herself. Her book had me hook, line, and sinker. What struck me most was the thread of "refreshingly unfussy bonds" woven throughout the text. Her family's decision to stick around and hush up was rewarded with common kinship, the daily hellos and flickers of warmth that ground us and make life richer. Her experience resonated deeply with my own.

We were welcomed by people who come from different places and speak different languages. But more than that, we lived the essential ordinariness of showing up to and sharing ownership of the same common space. My kids ate free cafeteria lunch with their friends and ran around at recess until they were all the same sort of sweaty. (Nothing levels the playing field like playing together on an actual field.)

It was obvious from the start: our desires are the same. We want the freedom and room to learn without barriers. We want to create. To laugh. We want to be teachers, to gather up our abundant gifts and fling them over each other. (Just thinking about the ways the school carries and serves us forms a lump in my throat—my signal that I should remain as close to it as possible.)

Ready for Action

Days before this last school year started, I received an apologetic email asking if our church, which sits across the street from the school, could supply notebooks to returning students. Budget cuts had left this essential uncovered and they were feeling a bit desperate.

Time was running short, so I called back and asked how many notebooks were needed. She hesitated for a beat. "We need twelve hundred total. But another church already promised two hundred. Whatever you're able to collect will be helpful."

I made a few more calls to track down the best deal then set out with my kids to buy and load one thousand notebooks into the back of our minivan.

The logistics were simple. Even the cost ended up being more accessible than I first imagined. In the grand scheme of things, buying a couple hundred dollars' worth of supplies for the school that helped raise my children didn't make a dent in the debt I owed.

Afterward I was tempted to dust off my hands and move on. But if I had chosen that route, I'd have missed the best part.

The next Sunday, I retroactively brought the need to our humble, charmingly uncool church. I shared the need and invited anyone interested in contributing to find me after the service.

The man sitting behind me, someone who has suffered crushing losses in recent years, passed me some cash. A St. Mark's founding mother slipped me a crisp bill folded neatly into quarters. A few others asked for my Venmo. I was already flooded with gratitude over the collective response—and that was before Dan found me.

Dan had joined our congregation while incarcerated at the neighborhood work release facility and the two of us hadn't yet officially met. "This is for the kids," he said quietly, reaching out his hand.

He dropped five one-dollar coins into my palm and made his way to the door.

I don't know the details of his life, but surviving a place famous for bleeding people dry, one that loves punishment and power-mongering more than actual reform, cannot be easy.

Gregory Boyle writes, "Here is what we seek: a compassion that can stand in awe at what the poor have to carry rather than stand in judgment of how they carry it."[6]

Those who the world labels "problems" are very often part of the solution. Those we see as needy often stand by ready to teach us something about generosity.

I'm learning what it looks like to live ready for practical

action. Sometimes it looks like a man wearing a faded heavy metal T-shirt and an ankle monitor emptying his pockets on short notice for the sake of his neighbor.

The Village

After Cal's fateful bike accident, I formed a friendship with Leah, the woman who'd come to his rescue. I was trimming a haul of green beans at my station at work when she called me for the first time.

"I have the strangest question and I couldn't think of anyone else to ask," she began.

On her morning walk, an unfamiliar man had approached her near the library and asked if he could make a call from her phone. His name was Jim. He had just been released from prison after serving four years. He'd walked eight miles from the county jail but had no phone and no way to get himself to the factory job waiting for him later that day.

Leah was paying attention, alert to what was happening around her, and willing, once again, to enter in. It would have been easy to dismiss him, especially after learning about his past. She could have left it at a polite smile and a half-hearted, "I'm sorry," something I have done many times. Instead, she made it her business, even though she wasn't sure what to do or how to help.

Unfortunately I was just as uncertain. I found Mike stocking dry cereal down the hall, and asked if he had any ideas.

"I could give him a ride, but my car isn't here."

I handed him the keys to my van and off he went.

A few hours later, he returned with an update. He'd set

Jim up with a prepaid phone and dropped him off at work. Jim had a place to stay for the next few nights, but his cash was still tied up at the prison that had released him and he had no immediate access to a kitchen. "He's going to be okay, but I'm worried about how he'll eat," Mike said.

Our kitchen manager got to work packing a box filled with ready-to-eat food, bottled water, and toiletries. That night after dinner, Cory delivered the box.

I can't help but wonder what the world would look like—what it would *feel* like—if we were quicker to notice, faster to care, and more eager to link arms and lift our weary neighbors over the hurdles?

I don't know what will become of Jim.

My hope is that he'll find his way, gathering his own band of trusted souls who will meet him in the streets of his hardest days and offer what they can.

An Incomplete List of Tips for Everyday Activism

Sister Helen Prejean said, "Being kind in an unjust system is not enough."[7] Learning to take action toward the work we believe in makes "issues" less hypothetical and abstract. But this shift from thoughts and prayers to actual movement, though necessary, is not easy. Sarah, my friend since we were fifteen, put it this way: "Doing a Good Samaritan deed can be stressful, worrisome, and make you want to puke."

Why do we resist? Because we're tired. Busy. Afraid of doing something wrong. We might be a tinge self-centered (insert gritting-teeth emoji). We're scared. We think it has to be personal in order for us to care. The list is hefty.

We need to begin anyway. Here are some tips to get started.

1. **Set the intention.** Defaulting to being over-whelmed, choosing to look away, opting out, or "focusing on joy," are privileges not everyone has. We won't ever find our way to "together" if we're not willing to dive into what's broken.

2. **Expect mistakes.** It's important we stay focused on educating ourselves so that we don't end up running around recklessly, making a bigger mess of things. Even still, we need to make peace with our inevitable blunders along the way.

3. **Do your homework.** Googling is a valid and valuable practice. On our journey to learn and unlearn, we cannot expect to be spoon-fed. Earmark some of your phone time for growth, not just entertainment or mindless scrolling. Follow experts and educators. Buy their books. Take their courses. Pay them for their expertise, recognizing their labor comes at a personal cost to them.

4. **Stay curious.** Read multiple (legitimate) news sources.[vi] Read things you disagree with. Cultivate relationships with safe people who might see the world a bit differently, not to change their minds but to learn.

vi. If something seems "off" about a story (i.e., no primary sources, a funky URL, overly dramatic language, few direct quotes), this is one of my favorite tools to gauge legitimacy: https://www.factcheck.org/.

5. **Receive critique.** In my anti-racism advocacy, I've given a few close BIPOC friends carte blanche to call me out whenever they see fit.[vii] However, there's a difference between leaving the door open for honest conversation with an established friend and expecting our friends or acquaintances to bear the burden of our education in their free time. Our education is *our* responsibility.

6. **Apologize.** Over and over. Again and again. The book *Minor Feelings* notes the importance of apologizing without self-serving guilt, which requires absolution from the person we hurt and places the emphasis back on our needs.[8] When we realize we have been wrong, a sincere apology should be offered with no strings attached.

7. **Make the change.** When we know better, we must do better.

8. **Speak up.** Though "preaching" is not our end goal, raising our voices about things that are unjust or unfair is a good starting point. Just remember, there's far more to speaking up than posting something online. In order for it to be more than performance art, it should lead to rooted action. We can speak up at a city council or neighborhood association meeting about predatory landlords or oppressive systems that force vulnerable people out. We can ask our school boards and faith leaders

vii. My friend Sharday uses the phrase "call in" rather than "call out." This gentle, generous posture helps form hard conversations into true moments of relational growth.

for better policies against racism. We can challenge our neighbor, family member, or coworker when they speak callously about issues that matter deeply to our BIPOC friends. We can even speak up to the owners of our local antique shop and ask them why they allow the sale of icons that profit from the perpetuation of oppression against BIPOC people.

9. **Get better at going bigger.** It's important to resist locally but equally important to do what we can to disrupt toxic systems around us. Follow candidates and vote in local elections. Run for office. Sign petitions. Contact politicians.[viii] March. Protest. When done collectively, these actions can and do bring about actual change.

10. **Get comfortable with discomfort.** We keep coming back to this. Even the smallest actions require something of us. They disrupt our "negative peace, which is the absence of tension," and this disruption is necessary to arrive at a "positive peace, which is the presence of justice."[9] Deidra Riggs shared this quote with me, and it applies to all of us newbie activists: "Scared is how you're feeling. Brave is what you're doing."

11. **Stay in it.** When people tell you your activism is creating division, remind them injustice itself is what divides us. Stay in it. When you max out, take

---

viii. I'm not much of a crier, but I always get choked up when I make these calls. It's a strange and vulnerable feeling I'd honestly rather avoid. Let's do it anyway.

a break. But stay in it. When people talk smack or even walk away? Stay in it.

Up-Close Admiration Society

Walking to school one afternoon to pick Silas up, I watched as a car crept through the intersection toward the orange-vested crossing guard and came to a stop beside her. A look of confusion passed over the crossing guard's face. I picked up my pace, nosy as ever.

Through the car's opened window, a dozen red roses emerged. The crossing guard accepted the flowers, stunned speechless. The car drove away.

She stood clutching the bouquet as I approached.

"Who was that?" I laughed.

"I have no idea. They just thanked me for being here every day."

Here's the thing. I regularly muse about doing this kind of rogue appreciation mission. For years I'd held profound gratitude for her, specifically, and for every school crossing guard across our city. They bring lawn chairs, pack water bottles, wrap scarves around their faces in February, all in the name of securing safe passage for children. I drive past them slowly, hoping my smile somehow conveys my gratitude.

Maybe it really does come through. Maybe they feel it.

They wouldn't miss it if it were roses.

I'm not suggesting we all install refrigerated flower coolers in the backs of our minivans and throw daisies or tulips at unsuspecting heroes.[ix] Brought into the mainstream, it would probably be a safety hazard, for starters.

I'd just like us to find our own weird ways of prying the good intentions from our minds and wearing them out into the world, our actual hearts on our actual sleeves. Kind words typed on the internet can be a buffer against our snarkiest, meanest siblings, who lack the basic understanding that we really are tied to each other, and that's a voyage that should not be abandoned. Let's just remember it's no replacement for real-life connection.

Tangibles matter. Showing up matters.

When bizarre ideas flit across our consciences, let's stop snuffing them out. No more thoughts of *That would be weird* or *It might make them uncomfortable.* I have never felt discomfited from being on the receiving end of practical kindness.

Podcaster and community evangelist Erin Moon writes, "[Doing] something small will not only push against the overwhelming tide of darkness in the world, but it will push against the same tide threatening to overwhelm you."[10]

It's all flowers. Every gesture. Every meal. Every offer of help. Every ride. Every apology. Every text. Every surprise chai latte. Every truthful word. Every hug in the dark beneath busted streetlights.

Each day is a question waiting to be answered.

Will we be an observer? Or a participant?

Connection awaits. It's so much simpler than we thought.

---

ix. Though I'm also not *not* suggesting it, because it sounds pretty fun.

ONE SIMPLE WAY
to Live as Neighbors

Spend some time thinking about what bubbles up inside you, makes you emotional in some way, or just makes you feel more alive. We often don't create enough space to be curious about ourselves, which is the very thing that can direct our way forward.

Take your time. Jot some notes. Once you've identified what gets you right in the feels, keep going. Are there any obvious bridges between that issue/idea and people already doing the work? Find them. Say hello. Resist the urge to start something new and join something that's already on the move.

If that feels bigger than what you're ready for, start by following two new voices on social media who speak into the particular issue of your heart. If they've written a book or designed an instructional course, buy it. (And then read it.)[x]

---

x. I'm a chronic over-buyer of books and overly optimistic about reading time, so my TBR pile is tall. But seriously, we can't learn from a book we don't read.

CHAPTER 9

Roots > Wheels

We recognize that staying put is our love song for the long haul.

EVERY YEAR WE'VE LIVED IN THIS HOUSE, we've made an effort to plant a small garden. A few scattered seeds, some herbs, a couple of leftover tomato and pepper plants passed along from my dad.

For me, it has always been more about the *idea* of a garden than anything, the miracle of watching things grow, whole meals sprouting up from neglected, underloved dirt. Sturdy zucchinis, peppers so plentiful the branches bow from their weight, Thai basil that far outpaces our capacity for summer curry.

I love gardening. In theory.

By early July, before the getting even gets good, my interest withers. I admit I enjoy daydreaming about my Jimmy Nardello peppers ripening to a deep crimson far more than

I enjoy watering them. The short walk beneath an unrelenting sun suddenly seems a bridge too far.

The 2020 growing season was different.

Hunkered down in the first months of the pandemic, as our kids stared at laptop screens through blue light–blocking glasses and Cory processed his absence from the jail by learning biblical Greek, we set out to plant our garden with a detailed plan and more intention than ever.

We rented a sod cutter and funneled our stimulus money toward a dump truck of pea gravel. We bought the mushroom compost recommended by Dwight Garber from Pleasant Hill, Ohio.[i] As usual we crowded the garden beds, but for the first time I penciled a diagram into my notebook in order to avoid the pitfall of overzealous, boredom-induced "weeding."[ii]

My garden thrived like never before, but I don't think it was the gravel border or even the luxe compost. For the first time, we were gardening with attention—which is to say we were gardening as intended. Through the critical heat spikes of July, we were there with our hand on the spigot. Being near and staying obsessed were their own reward. And then the actual treasure arrived.

I traipsed out in the mornings, barefooted, to take glamour shots of leggy flowering cosmos. I drummed up new recipes for our profusion of Sungold cherry tomatoes. I

---

i. This is how my dad introduces himself over the phone (a landline, naturally). Also, for many years, he somehow had a direct line to an elusive Amazon employee named Ben, who processed his orders over the telephone.

ii. Wherein I accidentally pull up all of my diablo cosmos because I convince myself they're weeds.

brined cucumber pickles in the middle of lazy, sun-shocked afternoons.

What started as four boxes of old dirt became a place of comfort, curiosity, and dinner. The wilder it grew the more I loved it.

I've come to see that this also applies to my family. My neighborhood. My church. My community.

Tidiness is overrated. If you don't believe me just ask the volunteer dill growing straight through the tangled zinnia stems, unbothered and somehow better for it. I let the garden do what it wanted. As it turned out, what it wanted most was to hold my attention.

I once made the bold proclamation that all I needed to know about science was learned from deglazing a pan, a literal hot take that I now recognize as a bit overbaked.[iii] Even so, I'm perfectly comfortable saying much of what we need to know about growing strong communities can be learned by tossing seeds into the mud.

Specifically—

Grow roots.

Be patient for a long time, through the sun and the rain.

Commit without expectation.

Hope to be surprised.

As we pursue a rhythm of simple connection in our lives, this is what it takes to make it work for the long haul. *But*

iii. Absolutely couldn't help it.

what even is a long haul? How long is long enough? Am I locking myself into a particular place/friend group/community . . . forever?

Excellent questions.

Growing Roots

Everyone's long haul looks a little different. Back on the farm I once waxed poetic on my blog that I was "never leaving." I meant it from the depths of my soul. I was content. Happy. I was living the life I'd always wanted. I couldn't imagine a better option.

Two years after I wrote that post, we packed it all up and moved. I learned to never say never. But in the years that followed I also learned community grows richer over time. I grew captivated by the thought of a future rooted in simply sticking around.

There's a level of privilege in this long-haul perspective. Not everyone has control over where they stay and when they go. From the ones who live at a landlord's mercy through a national housing crisis to those on the hunt for a more affordable or convenient option—there are lots of reasons why "long haul" is relative.

Additionally, things change. Jobs change. Family needs change. There's nothing wrong with packing up and moving to San Diego because you suddenly realize with searing clarity that you cannot endure one more winter battling Indiana's lake effect snow.

"Staying forever" is not always in the cards. The goal is

to belong to our particular people and place for as long as we're able. We can surrender to life's whims *and* put down roots along the way. (After all, half of the plants in my garden got their start in someone else's.)

As one military spouse explained to me, "We don't have the luxury of long haul anything. But we connect wherever the military sends us. We have friends everywhere."[1]

Our root system steadies us, anchoring us to our patch of earth. It feeds us. It grows us into who we are. And, if and when we leave, it goes with us.

Gardens are a living emblem of commitment, and community itself is the best picture of a garden I can imagine. Until we go—we stay. On purpose and with grit.

On Patience + Rough Weather

On my first trip to the Pacific Northwest, I stayed for two nights in a small coastal town with cinematic views. Gleaming black-rock beaches, bands of fog hovering dreamlike. Quaint and moody, it was the backdrop for a fairy tale.

Which begs the question, Would a fairy tale have a laminated tsunami evacuation route taped to the refrigerator door? Because this one did. In red, twenty-point font, the optimistically cautious hosts warned renters that in the presence of an earthquake, they should be prepared to seek higher ground at a moment's notice. Essentially it said, "Run for your lives!"

Sometimes fairy tales are set on catastrophic fault lines.[iv]

---

iv. In this case, the Cascadia subduction zone.

Sometimes the tectonic plates of ordinary life cause rumbling or even rupture.

Though we'd rather not think about a wall of water heaving toward us while we're drinking organic vacation coffee, so to speak, we'd be wise to anticipate the potential hazards and have a plan in place.

Cranky Neighbors

Cranky neighbors come in two basic varieties. The first just wants to be left alone. Part of being a good neighbor is recognizing and honoring this. When it comes to my "favorite" low-key cranky neighbor, interactions are few and far between. I don't see him often, but when I do I smile and wave. About half the time he returns the gesture.

The hermit in me honors the hermit in him while casually keeping him in my line of vision.

Come December I push the boundaries in the interest of holly-jollyness and deliver a foil pan of cookies to him, just like I do for others. Crankiness does not make anyone special enough to miss out on salted toffee bark. He receives the gift in his usual quiet and wary manner, and that's perfectly all right.[v]

The second sort of cranky neighbor is one who might, for example, repay feeding his cat for a month with accusations so outlandish you'll find yourself retelling the story often.[vi]

---

v. Christmas Day 2020, a knock on our door. It was him, bearing a plastic grocery bag filled with oranges. "I wanted to give something to you this time," he said, and shuffled away. My heart exploded.

vi. "I believe you've been throwing drug paraphernalia in my yard," he said, to the perplexed jail chaplain wearing two wristwatches. (This last detail is mostly irrelevant but I'm glad to have snuck it in.)

It's a crowd-pleaser and a reminder that, as my friend Sarah would say, "All God's children got problems."

In these cases we keep a low profile. And if, say, I happen to see such a person grousing at another neighbor, especially if it's a child, I might nonchalantly go deadhead my zinnias at that opportune moment. (Never underestimate the watchful presence of a middle-aged woman wielding snippers.)

Everyday Conflict

I once observed two police officers on my street after one neighbor had freaked out that another neighbor was parking her car on what he considered "his" portion of the curb. (Never mind that the city owns the curbs along with the streets they border.) After the officers dispersed, this angry neighbor stomped over to the property line and hammered a metal stake into the grass, presumably to mark his territory.

I've caught wind of conflicts over loud music, late-night parties, and fireworks at 1:00 a.m. on July 10. There have been kid squabbles, blocked driveways, all manner of boring grievances.

I wonder, What if we chose to see these regular inconveniences as bridges rather than fences? What if, instead of losing our minds over moonlight discos or other forms of rowdy celebration, we just thought, *That sounds fun!* and turned up our white noise app?

Granted, I remember trying to coax babies and anxious toddlers to sleep. These scenarios have different implications for different people. But is there something we could try first rather than jumping straight to "call the police"? Could we dare to simply walk next door and kindly state our case?

Other options exist before inviting strangers wearing guns to intervene on our behalf. Data shows that police presence in reported conflict is especially risky for neighbors of color.[vii] This is one more reason it matters to build relationships in peaceable times. Creating a culture of peace and learning to triage effectively is slow but worthy work. Tiny friendly encounters pave the way for when problems arise and we need a solid foundation of trust. Most dicey situations can be resolved with eye contact and honest words. Hopefully by now we've made enough peace with awkwardness to do what must be done. The people around us are not inconsequential. We'll be together until we aren't, with any luck long enough for our roots and wishes to tangle underground.

The Big "Boundaries" Talk

Walking with real people through the burned bridges and jump-scares of daily life guarantees a few solid perks. Kindness. Kinship. A bottomless fount of humor. It's the recipe

---

vii. A 2020 study of nearly 5,500 reported police-related deaths revealed that Black people are three times as likely to be killed during a police encounter than White people. In certain cities, the disparity more than doubled. See "Black People More Than Three Times as Likely as White People to Be Killed during a Police Encounter," Harvard School of Public Health, accessed February 2, 2022, https://www.hsph.harvard.edu/news/hsph-in-the-news/blacks-whites-police-deaths-disparity/.

for a brighter life. We were made to be warmed by the light of each other.

But there will be times when what was intended as a cozy glow gets stoked into a raging brushfire. Which is a poetic way of saying that sometimes the very people who punch up the flavor and fun will also completely wear us out.

This is the boundaries talk. We need them.

Trade Obligation for Honesty

My hair was on fire, so to speak, when we first landed in the neighborhood. More warm bodies mean more complications. This isn't a personal judgment against anyone in particular. It's just math. For example, one Shannan is a lot. One hundred Shannans would drain anyone's reserves. Living as a committed neighbor does not have to trap us in a chaos cyclone.

If I could only share one word of wisdom here, it would be this: saying no builds trust.

I'm serious.

If we allow every "emergency" to become our own, we are forgetting our place as companions and casting ourselves as saviors instead. No one wants to be saved. No one is asking for that. When we jump to a different conclusion, behaving as though we hold the keys to someone else's problem, trust erodes.

Here's what I mean. I have a friend who doesn't have a driver's license. My nearness to her and other nondrivers has opened my eyes to the hardship this often presents. A ride is often something I can easily provide.

But I came to see there were only so many times I could drop what I was doing at a moment's notice before resentment took over. Her level of need was not sustainable for me over time. I knew her circumstances would not be different for the foreseeable future, and I panicked a bit that she was starting to assume I'd always be available. At the same time I cherished her friendship and wanted to continue to help when I was able.

I gave myself permission to halt my reflexive *yes* response and instead pledged honesty. Real connections thrive best under the daylight of truth.

We should build our resilience for pushing past feelings of self-protection or control. While *no* is often my first impulse when interruptions pop up, connection means surrendering more easily to *yes*.

But if we find ourselves jotting strange mental notes about who's asking, how often, and how lopsided the "score" is, that's our sign to regroup. We need to have our *no* plan ready.

Here's mine. "I can't help right now. But please ask me every time. I will say yes if I can help, and I'll be honest when I can't."[viii]

In the years since, I've refined and practiced my *no* response, and I've gotten skilled at using it. Want to know what has happened? My resentment has faded away. My relationships have strengthened.

Saying no levels out uneven power dynamics. We go from

---

viii. "I can't" means anything from "I'm working," to "I have another appointment," to "The car is in the shop," to "I'm currently busy reading a novel on the couch in the middle of the afternoon."

feeling like a poorly run nonprofit to an actual friend with needs, obligations, desires, and crises of our own.

Saying no swaps obligation for authenticity.

When we recalibrate our relational compass to compassionate truth-telling, everyone wins.

Rest and Recovery

Have I mentioned I'm an introvert?[ix]

As we think about our plan for staying in close formation with the people near us, however long that ends up being, we're going to need a moment's rest. Or ten.

The popular lingo for this is *self-care*, though I have an emotional allergy to that term. It sounds so upscale. Too precious.

Beach vacations are great and I've heard good things about spa days, but that's not what this is about. Because our eye is naturally fixed on the daily grind, it only makes sense to pull our ideas about rest and recovery out of the clouds and wrestle them down to street level, where they're free for the taking.

We're finite people with limited physiological resources. For starters, let's be realistic about our human need for regular, ample sleep and act accordingly.

We also need old-fashioned downtime. Time to just be. To reclaim a portion of the joy and peace that might have gotten lost along the way.

Full disclosure: I'm terrible at finding the right balance between the two, too often choosing rest at the expense

ix. YES, SHANNAN.

of sleep. I'm working on that. But until I find a foolproof method, I seem to have landed on a respectable sleep/rest hybrid. It might sound dramatic, but a couple times a year, usually during winter, I hibernate. When I find myself casually jealous of someone who comes down with what I like to call a "cozy cold," that's my signal to skip the stuffy nose and sign myself up for the stage-set "cozy cold" experience. I call it Recovery Day, which is code for "staying in bed all day."

My early symptoms are always physical exhaustion paired with a frayed emotional state. I'm tired or sad or a combo of both and experience sudden kinship with my coworker from twenty years ago who once called our manager to say he wouldn't be in that day because he'd been afflicted with "the blues."

The "why" isn't really the point. This opt-out is about taking the space to replenish what's been depleted. Since I'm officially "It's too loud" years old, for me this usually means silence and time to zone out. No problem-solving. No chores. Minimal word expenditure. On this rare day, these things are not my concern.

Years of perfecting Recovery Day have provided me with a few general guidelines: nonbinding fabrics only, a stack of reading material nearby (fiction, if possible, as this is not the day for bad news or learning), good snacks, naps as needed. Am I available to referee video game disputes? Absolutely not. Can I give you a ride? "I can't help right now. But please ask me every time." Showering is optional, required only if it happens to speak to my heart in some way. Food will still very much speak to my heart, but I'm not cooking.[x]

Not everyone is the "stay in bed all day" type[xi] like me. I don't have young children or other people who require my constant care and attention at this juncture. All I'm saying is that when our hearts are weary and our brains are tired, we need to find ways—even the smallest of ways—to recover. This really isn't optional.

In the book *24/6*, Tiffany Shlain lays out her family's rhythm of a weekly "Tech Shabbat."[2] Calling to her Jewish heritage, they set aside twenty-four hours each week to fall off the grid, turning away from screens and tech in order to feel the oozy, delicious slowing of time. This tradition kicks off with roast chicken and challah by candlelight, which they often enjoy with friends. They spend the remainder of their shabbat[xii] napping, journaling, spending time outdoors, and focusing on creating rather than producing.

After a few years of haphazardly trying to institute phone-free Sundays, I've embraced this Tech Shabbat with a sleepy zeal. At first the Martin teenagers attempted to throw us off course with a few modern-day examples of garment rending and pouring ashes on their heads, but the benefits were so obvious we pushed through, giving their antics all of our disregard. One recent Sunday I quietly noted that Cal offered to cook dinner, Ruby practiced her cello without being reminded, and Silas worked on his

---

x. On my last Recovery Day, Ruby baked cookies. I blessed her efforts, shouted answers to her questions from my rest nest, and requested bedside delivery.

xi. Tell me you're a sloth without telling me you're a sloth.

xii. Shabbat is the Hebrew word for "sabbath," which means a day of rest and worship.

budding candle-making business for hours. Being bored shows us what we're made of. (Guess what? We're made of really cool, creative stuff.)

Our family's version of shabbat is remarkably less cute than candlelight and fresh-baked challah, but we're coming home to the fact that a shared snack before bed or a couple extra hours to read are suitable counterweights to the slog of being human.

We can't always spend a whole day in bed, but most of us can spend a day (or part of one) taking a break from the noise in order to hear the song. Whatever our resting looks like, if it results in being less covetous of our neighbor's scratchy throat, I call it a win.

Commit without Expectation

We have a framed print in our home of this quote from Hellen Keller: "Life is either a daring adventure or nothing."[3]

To be clear, living with arms wide, palms up, our hearts on our sleeves, and our front doors easy on their hinges is a recipe for daring adventure. It offers no guarantees.

We will perpetually let each other down. We'll get it wrong. We'll learn to apologize faster and more sincerely.

And we can't control how others choose to react or behave. The universe does not promise a wide berth around toxic people. At times we'll go out on a limb only to wind up disappointed—and sometimes still alone.

These are the unvarnished facts. But this is the long game. It's unhurried work. The sun will keep rising. Our roots are never wasted.

Examining the Rhizosphere

There's a name for the study of plant roots: *rhizology*. Rhizologists are scientists who study the rhizosphere—the area of soil surrounding plant roots, essentially a root system's natural habitat. Their research yields some fascinating conclusions. For example, when comparing root growth beneath porous versus nonporous asphalt, one study concluded, "Root growth was found to be much denser and deeper in the soil under the porous asphalt presumably because of greater access to water. Additionally, tree growth above the porous asphalt was also improved."[4]

Basically roots, along with their vegetation, grow thickest when left a bit exposed to the elements. Nature echoes the sentiments of songwriter Leonard Cohen, "There's a crack in everything. . . . That's how the light gets in."[5]

The metaphors between urban ecology and community are ripe for the picking. For now, let's do some examining of our own.

Last summer, after the improbable delight of being caught in a rogue rainstorm on our neighbor's patio as we were enjoying the best tacos of my life, I wrote these words:

> We aren't BFFs with all of our neighbors. We don't go on vacations together. We haven't been inside each other's homes more than a dozen times. (Backyards and patios are another story.) But we water each other's flowers and check each other's mail. We borrow ladders and limes. We have each other's backs. They shape who I am and how I see. At times, I've fantasized about new places and a different house but in the end, these faces and names are the reason I won't

go. We belong here. Side by side, with so many memories together. It can be awkward. Also necessary, and good. I can't quit the thought that if more of us would inch toward each other for the long haul, our lives would feel sturdier.[6]

Readers began adding their own stories, their own roots.[xiii]

Today one of my neighbors at my apartment complex had a cast taken off his arm. We all keep our windows and doors open here because it is in the seventies almost constantly. He always quietly walks from his door down to his car, rarely initiating conversations. Today, one neighbor saw him and called out from his living room, "Hey, look at you! You're healed!" Several of us followed suit. This introverted man stopped and basked in our notice, beaming from ear-to-ear. He lifted both arms and turned slowly so we could all see, and at the end of his slow twirl he danced up and down like a boxer who just won a fight, saying, "It feels so good to be healed!"[7]

My parents met friends throughout their military time and remained in contact for decades until death separated them.[8]

There's something comforting about knowing my neighbor will spot a package lying on my porch and tuck it safely around back or bring in my garbage can when I'm away.[9]

Years ago, a new neighbor moved in beside us. We introduced ourselves to one another. He shared with me that his mother raised him to believe our neighbors are our most

xiii. Some comments have been edited for clarity.

valued extended family that we don't (usually) get to choose. In an emergency, they're most likely the first people who will be there before anyone else. Before emergency personnel and before our blood family. They might save our home, our life, or the life of someone we love. So treat them as you would treat anyone who holds such an important role in your life. We moved away a few years later and left that neighborhood behind. But what he said has never left me.[10]

Just last night our neighbor texted me that we had left our garage door open. I love my neighbors![11]

A new baby was born, amid the maxed-out COVID hospital last week. And a whole block rejoiced.[12]

There in the rhizosphere was living proof of what happens when we stay open and porous, sharing the rain and letting each other in. Vivid portraits of lasting bonds and a sense of security. Evidence that every "no biggie" baby step stacks into the sort of big deal that will make a stoic woman in Goshen, Indiana, weepy.

The best stuff emerges from the hidden in-between, sometimes between moments of literal sunshine and rain. This sense of wholeness doesn't happen apart from our actual lives but *within* them.

In her magnificent book *Braiding Sweetgrass*, Indigenous author and scientist Robin Wall Kimmerer writes about "The Council of Pecans,"[xiv] in which pecan groves statewide

---

xiv. Elizabeth Gilbert describes *Braiding Sweetgrass* as "A hymn of love to the world." That's the goal here: to find the tune and keep singing it.

bear their fruit in unison. Some researchers attribute this phenomenon to pheromones that journey through the air, delivering messages of safety or doom to the sisterhood. Others believe signals are whispered underground, through root systems. Either way,

> If one tree fruits, they all fruit—there are no soloists. . . . The trees act not as individuals, but somehow as a collective. Exactly how they do this, we don't yet know. But what we see is the power of unity. What happens to one happens to us all. We can starve together or feast together. All flourishing is mutual.[13]

What more could we ask for?

Hope to Be Surprised

Once a month, I follow the same path to an evening church council meeting. Heading out for one such meeting, I considered taking a different route only to be pulled toward the potholed alley lined with plastic garbage cans. Cicadas sang along to August's unrelenting heat. Weeds disguised as beauty scrambled up telephone poles. Like usual familiarity brought a poetic sort of solace. *I know this place and it knows me.* An empty chip bag tumbled along the asphalt before me, leading the way.

I checked my watch, proud that I would arrive an uncharacteristic five minutes early.

Twenty paces later, a neighbor stepped into the alley from his backyard. "It's so hot!" he said, grinning. I pushed my sweaty bangs off my face in agreement. "The breeze helps a little," he continued. I motioned toward the small spot of shade being cast into the yard and offered my agreement. "The shade is nice."

Two strangers, forming simple sentences to span a slight language barrier, talking about the weather. Somehow it was the opposite of small talk.

We both veered into the yard, where enormous terra cotta pots held zinnias and marigolds that towered over our heads. Over the years I'd stopped many times to snap a photo of his cheery, school-bus-yellow home. It's among the surest signs of life in our neighborhood through the gray slog of winter. Come summertime the yard joins the community color show.

He called through the back door to ask his wife to join us, and she did. "She doesn't speak English, but she can understand. She used to see you walking your kids to school. She remembers you," he said. (More evidence that those short walks and simple hellos really do matter.) He helped the two of us chat about her showstopping flowers but also about the butterflies and bees working hard to keep us fed.

I knew the council meeting had begun yet I couldn't tear myself away—not from the hollyhocks, not from these kindhearted folks who had just unceremoniously invited me into their personal space, promising seeds at summer's end if I wanted them.

Eventually I thanked them and said goodbye, pledging to stop by again.

He met my eyes and smiled. "Maybe one day you and my wife can walk together."[xv]

Back home after the meeting, I heard a knock at the door. Josh stood on the other side, his moped parked in our driveway. We'd met him years ago when he would occasionally pop in for the free dinner our church hosted on Wednesday nights.

Since then he has eaten tomato soup at our kitchen table and caught up with us on our porch. He goes dark for long stretches of time, sometimes turning up at the jail where Cory works.

The years have gone by. Cory's beard is grayer and I find myself staring at my reflection in the mirror sometimes, pulling the sides of my face back for a glimpse of who I used to be. Josh, meanwhile, appears to be eternally seventeen. "I have a soft spot for him," I've said more than once. Seeing his face unexpectedly at our door is always proof that connection has the final say.

On that sticky August night Cory wasn't home. "Tell him to hit me up on Facebook." Josh smiled, staring at his shoes as usual. "I'll come back again soon."

Two interactions, two hours apart. Both were reminders of what happens when we stick around for as long as we can. We suffer fickle hearts and good intentions gone bad. Our attention spans contract. We surrender to boredom and forget the greenness of the grass beneath our feet. We're humans fighting the same old human conditions. The

---

xv. The first thing I did when I got home that night was type their names into my illustrious "neighbor" email file. We remember these details when we don't allow ourselves excuses to forget.

culture might not value the slow bloom of steady growth and enduring presence, but we know better.

The magic isn't what happens *when* we stay. The magic *is* the staying, the sticking around even when we feel restless.

We create homes and plan to stay.[xvi] We plant carrots, peonies, and a tree, if we're able. We find comfort in the shade of each other. We feast on forgiveness and common ground.

Every year at summer's end, around the time the kids return to school and we swap fireflies for familiar routines, our blackberry vines reach out and our neighbors' black-eyed Susans reach back, holding hands.

Creation keeps showing us how to be human.

Here's to taking the long road and laying down roots. Here's to staying until we go. Here's to penning some memories in ink, to remembering where the floors creak and the sidewalks buckle, to chasing the memory of a scent back through time and lingering there, to tattooing *home* on our hearts and carrying it with us from house to house, from year to year, from then to now and back again.

ONE SIMPLE WAY
to Live as Neighbors

Till up a little patch of earth or grab a pot and a bag of soil and plant some seeds. Lettuce or spinach are easy and

xvi. Jeremiah 29:7.

tolerate cooler weather before summer saps the will right out of us. Carrots are another easy option and nothing beats the thrill of pulling a fresh one from the ground. Find something you like or try something new. Pay close attention to what the practice requires from you and what it offers back.

The process and the waiting are gifts in themselves.

If you end up growing actual food (what a miracle!) share some with a neighbor for extra credit.

CHAPTER 10

Empathy > Everything

> We commit to loving our neighbor as ourselves—
> quick to empathize, slow to judge, ready to be
> wowed.

It was a late-January morning, snow-glazed, with the sort of air that reaches into your lungs and yanks as the sun pinks through the atmosphere. Warm then cold. Soft and sharp. Mercies new.

We made our commute across town to Silas's school: around the bend, past the CVS and the library. I always dreaded the next landmark: along the sidewalk a neighbor had erected huge wooden signs scrawled with vicious political messages.

Day after day, I'd watched from my peripheral vision as my sensitive son turned his head to take them in. I wished for the younger years, when we'd held hands on the short and peaceful walk to school. Back then he would occasionally blurt out a prayer, thanking God for the trees or asking for help for the day ahead. It always surprised me. But shoes and playgrounds aren't the only things we outgrow as we maneuver through a world that long ago stopped trying to live up to its children. We take up armor. Our hope gets rusty.

Si is a feeler. An empath. He's the one who rubs slow circles of compassion over the backs of the brokenhearted. He stays, leaning heavily enough against the hurt that he ends up taking some away with him.

I tried not to draw attention to the sidewalk calamity. But on that particular winter day, my casual efforts were interrupted by his voice, a bit deeper than before, praying for our neighbor with the same generosity he'd once offered for the trees.

I didn't know what to say, so I simply told him his response was kind.

Silence.

Another red light.

And then he said, "I think she makes those signs because she has a lot of emotions inside and she feels like no one listens to her. I know what she feels like, in a dark part of me."

Don't we all?

We know what she feels like, somewhere, in a dark part of us.

The bigger question is, Do we care enough to remember this common ground when our eyes lock and we rattle with judgment, or worse?

In the wilds of connection empathy is our North Star.

The Possibility of Progress

Empathy is generally defined as the ability to put ourselves in someone else's shoes. It's the ability to see the world as others see it, avoid judgment, recognize the emotion of others, and communicate those emotions.[1]

Latasha Morrison describes empathy as being in it together, while sympathy happens from a safe distance.[2] It's the difference between pity and solidarity. Brené Brown adds that empathy "fuels connection" while sympathy "drives disconnection."[3] If we want to change the world (we do!) we have to get closer to each other. Until we do we'll stay stuck in our suspicions.

Over time the slow, persistent work to see one another as fully human—to devote ourselves to the experiment of mutual respect—will grow into something greater, something with teeth. It all leads us here to this place of sacred with-ness, real friendship, where we look around and realize we're not as alone as we once feared.

Author and scholar Dante Stewart writes,

> Loving people is not simply asking, "how can I be near to them?" It is all of us asking, "how can we love people by seeing them, hearing them, relishing in them, and creating a world where people feel loved, inspired, and protected?"[4]

Compassion is empathy with its shoes laced. It moves. Creates. As Danté said, it relishes.

Real talk: I'm not ready to relish the lady with the signs. Generally speaking, she vexes me. But I watch her waving to cars as they drive by, drilled into her chaos cause, and I have to wonder what might have left her feeling unloved or unprotected.

Compassionate empathy is not about offering blanket acceptance or absolution. We should never shrug off bad behavior. (In fact, it's time to get serious about the complicity of our silence in the face of cruelty.)

Facing our own hypocrisy and unkindness helps us understand each other. They're *in us*, just like Silas said. It's much harder to throw shade when we're acquainted with our own darkness. We aren't perfect and utopia is not our goal. But we're a little more open than we used to be.

Empathy believes progress is possible.

Forging Friendship Right Where We Are

It's time to liberate our dusty ideas about what friendship is and who it's for. We've gotten so used to the idea of moving through life with just our family and a tight circle of friends that we've lost our ability to imagine a wider web of connection encompassing a gorgeous mess of layers and levels of closeness.

What if *neighbor* is just another word for *friend*?

Courtney E. Martin is right: "You can be a functional, and even beloved, community without being close friends."[5] Regular, smiling, everyday "friends" is more than enough. Holding this frame up to the people around us is one more way to loosen any tension and knock the edges off our differences.

EMPATHY BELIEVES PROGRESS IS POSSIBLE.

To name one another "friend" is to identify, in some way, with each other. Friendship closes the gap for empathy. We might not completely understand what it means to be a neighbor (though we've made a ton of progress!) but we do know something about being a friend.

Here's a quick refresher of some key friendship goals, all of which can be applied to people we've known for decades and the folks we just met yesterday.

Be Safe

Trust tops the list. An easy way to gauge the safeness of relationships is to pay attention to how we speak about people when they aren't around. A friend who will casually tell me someone else's dirt will just as easily dispense mine.

Be Real

I want to see people as they really are, not as they wish they were. Life isn't perfect and we all struggle. It's no fun wondering if someone's taking mental notes on my relative put-togetherness. Share your doubts. Show me your messes and mistakes. I'll love you forever.

Offer the Benefit of the Doubt

If we're friends, it's just a matter of time before I say something stupid or let you down. I'll arrive late to dinner. I'll forget your birthday or miss your big news. This makes us human. Rather than being surprised or disappointed, let's extend the benefit of the doubt whenever possible.

Apologize

Having said that, a sincere apology goes a long way toward keeping friendships fortified and sturdy. We can be quick to say we're sorry at even the hint of a mess-up, valuing the relationship over our pride.

Tell the Whole Truth

Can we normalize not being "fine" or "good"? Most of life happens somewhere in the clash of stressed-to-the-max and bliss. It's complicated and we can say so, even when it's unpretty or scary or dicey or weird. If life is good, don't tamp it down. If life is hard, I can handle it. If I ask for your opinion it's because I really do need your signature wisdom and wit.

Safety + Flowers: A Short Story about Empathy

Act I

Back when my son Cal spent his first summer job as our dishwasher in The Window's kitchen, one of the lunchtime regulars was a quiet, kind man named Terry. It wasn't long before he wound up on the payroll, with a job in the food pantry across the hall. Head down. Still quiet. Getting the job done.

One afternoon, tasked with unloading a large donation from a local grocery store,[i] he wandered in and out of the

i. Weekly donations from local grocery stores are the lifeblood of our operation, along with farmers who bring dozens of eggs, urban optimists who arrive with garbage bags of cucumbers, and church ladies who bake cookies just because. It takes a village to feed a village.

kitchen bearing gifts. A huddle of perfect eggplants. A haul of carrots. Some random cream cheese. Things he knew we would use.

We crossed paths in the narrow hallway moments after his produce processional. Without a word, he handed me a frozen veggie pizza and a sleepy bouquet of grocery store mums. I don't remember much about the pizza but the flowers lived out the rest of their days in a mason jar on our kitchen table, a living memorial to the delight of human kindness.

Act II

Cal returned home after riding his bike to a friend's house. He'd been alone on the trail, anxiously aware of his seclusion. "But then I saw a couple of the homeless guys from work and I knew I was safe."[ii]

We've gotten to know many people and their different struggles and complexities through The Window. Some are unsheltered. Many are not. Regardless of the details, Cal and I have both seen, up close, the ways our society judges, and even criminalizes, those who experience material poverty.

Because of our mutual proximity, we know better. We have come to better know the luck of our draw as we live and work with and near people who've beat the odds—complicated, hardworking, exasperating, hilarious, loving people.

ii. Cal's word choice of *homeless* is common, but some better options are *unsheltered*, *unhoused*, or, in any case where housing status is not explicitly needed, just *person*.

We do our small part and they do theirs. What we have in the end is more safety. And some days more flowers.

The Perilous Promise of Hope

Our empathy grows and hope arrives with it. The closer we get the safer we are. The safer we are the braver we get. We want to belong to each other, to believe it's possible, to know beneath our armor and in our skin that we can do this thing. We begin to believe we're up to the task of sharing space in this puzzling labyrinth of beliefs and best wishes.

We can make it work. We don't have to carry on constantly baffled and half-hating each other. We don't have to accept a foreseeable future where people are grouped according to where they come from, how much they have, or who they know. We don't have to resign ourselves to a failed human experiment. We can write new hypotheses—watchful and steady, closed mouths and open doors—and put them to the test.

Hope sounds so sweet but it's a risky enterprise. In order for it to work it has to be available to everyone. Abundantly available. Inexhaustibly available. As ubiquitous as clouds in the sky.

Hope isn't just for the middle class or the decision makers. It wears no price tag and requires no password.

Until everyone has hope, no one does.

This means there's no amount of hope too little or too great. We don't get to split hairs and tell young men weighed down with systemic burdens they aren't hoping hard enough. We don't get to shake our heads at desperate families fleeing danger or desolation and say they're hoping too much.

In order for hope to be real it has to be free. No gatekeepers. No restraints.

Viewed from the contagion of empathy, there is no end to the capacity within us to root for, fight for, and hope for each other. We can offer the world around us what our own hearts crave.

I once assisted with tattoo removal inside the jail. My job was to point a stream of cold air over the skin to numb it as the technician directed the laser. The removal process is much more painful and time-intensive than the process of getting a tattoo, and I saw my share of tough guys sweating bullets and looking woozy. One man in the chair that day squeezed a stress ball to distract himself from the pain as past regrets shattered beneath his skin. Between the pops of the laser, he talked about his dreams of a do-over. "If you do what you did, you'll get what you got. I'm proof that's true. I'm ready to do things different this time," he said.

Our culture is churning, perpetually turbulent. For too long we've allowed ourselves to be swept into the undertow, believing we're not strong enough to swim against the currents of ego and angst.

We keep doing what we did. And we keep getting what we got.

Fracture. Division. Loneliness. Fear.

"All despair can make is more of itself," writes John Green.[6] Just like that man getting his tattoo removed, we want something more. So we grab hold of each other and swim toward the shore. We save our lives by sharing them. Former Army medic turned peacemaker Diana Oestreich says it well: "Loving our enemies is what transforms fear into freedom."[7]

Someone recently asked me, through tears, "What do you even mean by hope? I don't get it." Hope takes different shapes for different people. For me it's the sky. It's paying attention and noticing the one slim moment where I feel peace, or calm, or joy, or love. It's green beans in the garden. It's the belief that there's always more than what we see. It's telling the truth.

As the Chinese parable goes, "It is better to light one candle than curse the darkness."

Hope is the flickering belief that a flame is a flame is a flame.

Watching from the Sky

The night before I fly a low tremor of anxiety always settles over me. In jolts and flashes I acknowledge this could be the last time I kiss my family goodbye. (This is dramatic, yes, but so is hurtling through the air inside a metal bird.)

Once I make my way to the airport I hustle through security, find my gate, and settle in to observe my flight-mates. An elderly woman pulling crackers from her pocketbook, quietly passing one to her husband. A gruff guy in his fifties with a long ponytail and soft eyes. A young family with two strollers and a preschooler on a backpack leash, the mom expertly concealing her frazzled state with a bubbly tone. My anxiety unclenches. When I board my plane, I peek through the cockpit window, now and then surprised to see a woman in charge. The flight attendants smile. I smile back. And breathe.

Maybe the plane will go down. Probably not, but it could happen. (This is the anxiety talking.) If it does, we're going down together. This thought is a strange comfort. As I look from face to face, even the scowling ones, I can't help but think that surely our collective hope will keep us in the air.

Viewed from the sky, at midnight, the lives below look like stars, constellations of possibility. Galaxies of hope. This is the reverb of empathy, holding tightly to our shared role in this strange, exhilarating bid to belong together.

Clearing our sight line for each other is our essential project—a lifetime of small intentions.

If we want to know we're not alone we're going to have to keep pointing our feet in the direction of each other. We will retrace our steps until we wear down a path between us.

So many of us are trying to nudge the momentum of humanity toward the light. We're marching. Writing. Discussing. We're using our voices for worthy yeses and non-negotiable nos. We're praying. We are holding the ones we love close. We're reading words with meat on their bones. We're shutting our mouths. Finally, we are ready to listen.

Here we are. Together. For a while or forever. Entrusted to each other.

"Being scared will not get the work done," says novelist

Jennifer Longo.[8] We remember our hesitations, how they did us no favors, and search for better solutions. Cutting through the darkness, the clouds, the noise, we find ourselves staring at each other. Our loneliness recedes.

Love is not merely the absence of hate. It's salt and sweat, dirt and tears, the chemistry of endurance.

Living is messy work but hope keeps scrubbing us clean. Every morning. Every moment. It's in the leaves on the trees swaying in September's changing air, reminding us to be flexible and to let go. It's here in the play of an evening shadow across my kitchen cabinets, uncommon beauty when darkness passes over light. It's in the bubble of the pizza crust baking, bread for the journey.

Hope looks like home. It feels like patience and adventure. It's a song and we're all in it.

Yes, we can go out on a limb.

Yes, we can do that strange thing.

Yes, generosity is practical.

Yes, it can be honoring.

Yes, investing in the people near us is never wasted.

Yes, it counts.

Yes, it matters.

Yes, making our one little corner brighter makes the world brighter.

We don't pursue connection because we know it will be easy. We pursue connection because we believe it multiplies our possibilities for wholeness.

We believe the opposite of lost is free. We believe we can't be free on our own so we reach out, grab tight, and hold on for dear life.

To this we will testify.

ONE SIMPLE WAY
to Live as Neighbors

Connection is a circle, not a straight line. From attentiveness to empathy to hope, each feeds the others. I'm convinced staring at something small and beautiful might be the best way to survive this startling world.

Beauty is both freedom and fuel. Today, zoom in on the details of your ordinary, treasured life. Jot down a few sparks of beauty or delight. Search for them like an artist. Hold them in your hand. Read them like a poem. Fall in love.

I'll go first:

The sound of skateboards scratching down the street.

The breeze billowing the curtains at dusk.

A high school orchestra, in tuxes and long black
gowns, tuning their strings.

Your turn.

A Neighbor's Blessing

MAY YOU GO OUT into this bewildering world warmed by the fire of possibility.

May you come to see walking shoes, soup spoons, mini-vans, and wrinkled hands as worthy tools for connection.

May your heart stay tender, your hands stay open, and your door stay easy on its hinges.

May you find comfort in the moon, art in the clouds, and goodness in the faces around you.

May you gather, listen, and hope relentlessly.

And may you never give up on the living light of belonging, right where you are.

Grace and peace and gumption be with you.

Acknowledgments

START WITH HELLO would not exist without the people who believe we're better together and continue to ask, "Where do I start?" Thank you for pushing me to make the message as simple as possible. I love hearing about the small steps you've already taken, and I can't wait to see where we go from here.

Special thanks to *The Soup* (and *The Secret Soup*) subscribers. You're the reader-friends I turn to first with the backstories, the ruminations, and the snacks I'm hiding from my family. I appreciate you immensely, and I'll never stop saying so.

Without my actual community, there would be no story to tell. It is an extravagance of riches that there are too many people to name. To every person who has checked in on me, asked good questions, prayed for me, celebrated with me, and generally believed I had it in me to do this again, thank you.

Window kitchen crew, chopping veggies with you for

hours on end is my dream job and strangely fuels this other weird work I do. Thank you for having opinions about things like red pepper flakes and jicama. You're some of the smartest, kindest humans I know, and I'm obsessed with you.

Sarah Hughes and Kim Mack, even when the details might get hazy, you'll always be the Board of my dreams.

Goshen neighbors far and wide, we struck gold when we landed here. Thank you for teaching me how to live as a neighbor, and for supporting my complicated urge to write about it.

José Chiquito Galván, your feedback made this book clearer and kinder. I'm lucky to call you neighbor and honored to call you friend.

Grace Cho and Haverlee Ottley, my brilliant "ideal readers" and dear friends, thank you for your clear-eyed observations. (Let's hope for tea together soon!)

Emily P. Freeman, I would be an absolute disaster without you. Thank you for reminding me what's true and being my favorite co-imaginator.

Amber, Annie, Kat, Mariah, Natasha, Kendra, Grace, Bri, Deidra, Lisa-Jo, Megan (and so many more), thank you for reminding me that though I might work in my pajamas, I don't work alone.

Parish Collective family, you are the treasure I didn't know I needed. What a thrill to imagine and work alongside you.

Curtis and Karen Yates, you have my back always. Thank you for your giant, savvy hearts, your excellent ideas, and your determined belief that living as neighbors really will change the world.

Kelsey Bowen, thank you for grasping the vision early and being a fierce, fun champion (with treats up your sleeve!).

Andrea, Lindsey, Eileen, Wendy, and the rest of the Revell team, your enthusiasm has made all the difference. Thank you for being a dream come true.

Garber and Martin families, we grow and we change but we're still here, together. Thank you for the practical ways you help me along the way, and for proving that a shared faith and commitment to humor will carry us.

Cal, Ruby, Si, Robert, and Haven, thank you for thinking it's medium-cool that your mom is an author and for cheering me on even when it's not convenient. Your love has changed the way I see the world, and your fingerprints are all over everything I write. Watching you become is my favorite pastime. I love you forever.

Cory, it's fun to try to pinpoint how we ended up right here, in this particular life, but so much of it must be mystery, and I'm good with that as long as you're here. Thank you for being our steady roots. I love you. I can't wait to see what happens next.

Notes

Chapter 1 Awake > Asleep

1. Courtney E. Martin, *The New Better Off: Reinventing the American Dream* (Berkeley: Seal Press, 2016), 132.

2. Krista Tippett, "Michael Longley: The Vitality of Ordinary Things," *On Being with Krista Tippett* (podcast), November 3, 2016, https://onbeing .org/programs/the-vitality-of-ordinary-things/.

3. Simone Weil, "Letter to Joë Bousquet, 13 April 1942," in Simone Pétrement, *Simone Weil: A Life*, translated by Raymond Rosenthal (New York: Pantheon Books, 1976).

Chapter 2 Windows > Mirrors

1. "Make New Friends," ScoutSongs.com, accessed January 27, 2022, https://www.scoutsongs.com/lyrics/makenewfriends.html. Adapted from "Make New Friends but Keep the Old," by Welsh composer Joseph Parry (d. 1903). See Frank Bott, "Parry's 1894 American Tour," *Joseph Parry: Pencerdd America*, accessed January 27, 2022, http://josephparry .org/booksarticlestalks.htm#AmTour.

2. National Trust, "2009 National Trust Conference: Closing Plenary Session—Congressman John Lewis," recording, 35:35, accessed February 28, 2022, SoundCloud, https://soundcloud.com/preservationnation /2009-national-preservation-conference-john-lewis.

Chapter 3 Listening > Talking

1. Be A King (@BerniceKing), "If you're not working for justice," Twitter, May 30, 2020, https://twitter.com/BerniceKing/status/126659626 2985555968.

2. Amanda Gorman, "The Hill We Climb," *The Hill We Climb: An Inaugural Poem for the Country* (New York: Viking, 2021).

3. Martin Luther King Jr., as quoted in "Fake MLK Quote Goes Viral," *The Root*, May 3, 2011, https://www.theroot.com/fake-mlk-quote-goes -viral-1790863806.

4. Emily P. Freeman, "Episode 147: Be Anti-Racist," *The Next Right Thing* (podcast), October 6, 2020, https://emilypfreeman.com /?s=be+anti-racist&posttype_search=podcast.

5. Latasha Morrison (@latashamorrison), "Don't deflect," Instagram, June 4, 2020, https://www.instagram.com/p/CBBZuI6Bvou/.

6. Cami Zea (@zeaink), "You are my neighbor and I commit myself," Instagram, September 22, 2021, https://www.instagram.com /p/CUIb4q7JvWC/.

Chapter 4 Open Door > Perfect Décor

1. Myquillyn Smith (@thenester), "The size of your house," Instagram, August 26, 2021, https://www.instagram.com/p/CTCghu1r35M/.

Chapter 5 Familiar > Fussy

1. Bri McKoy, *Come and Eat: A Celebration of Love and Grace Around the Everyday Table* (Nashville: Thomas Nelson, 2017), 148.

2. Michael Wear, "Foreword," in Kaitlyn Schiess, *The Liturgy of Politics: Spiritual Formation for the Sake of Our Neighbor* (Downers Grove, IL: InterVarsity, 2020), 2.

3. Jemar Tisby, *The Color of Compromise: The Truth about the American Church's Complicity in Racism* (Grand Rapids: Zondervan, 2019), 15.

Chapter 6 Complexity > Comfort

1. Parker J. Palmer, *Let Your Life Speak: Listening for the Voice of Vocation* (San Francisco: Jossey-Bass, 1999), 99.

2. Palmer, *Let Your Life Speak*, 108.

3. Christa Wells, "Come Close Now," *Feed Your Soul* (Nashville: Zodlounge, 2013).

4. Clint Smith, *How the Word Is Passed: A Reckoning with the History of Slavery Across America* (New York: Little, Brown, 2021).

5. John Green, *The Anthropocene Reviewed: Essays on a Human-Centered Planet* (New York: Dutton, 2021), 7.

Chapter 7 Tender > Tough

1. Drew DeSilver, "Global Inequality: How the U.S. Compares," Pew Research Center, December 19, 2013, https://www.pewresearch.org/fact -tank/2013/12/19/global-inequality-how-the-u-s-compares/.

2. DeSilver, "Global Inequality."

3. Luke Gascho, "A Land Acknowledgement," Goshen College, November 13, 2019, https://www.goshen.edu/news/2019/11/13/a-land-acknowledgement/.

4. Schiess, *Liturgy of Politics*, 37.

5. Smith, *How the Word Is Passed*, 41.

6. Hanif Abdurraqib, *They Can't Kill Us Until They Kill Us: Essays* (Columbus, OH: Two Dollar Radio, 2017), 22.

7. Cole Arthur Riley (@blackliturgies), "If you wait to be unafraid," Instagram, May 10, 2021, https://www.instagram.com/p/COseh-8h9Jf/?utm_medium=copy_link.

8. Osheta Moore, *Dear White Peacemakers: Dismantling Racism with Grit and Grace* (Harrisonburg, VA: Herald Press, 2021), 64–65.

9. Gordon C. Nagayama Hall, "The Platinum Rule: Treat Others the Way They Wish to Be Treated," *Psychology Today*, February 7, 2017, https://www.psychologytoday.com/us/blog/life-in-the-intersection/201702/the-platinum-rule.

Chapter 8 Practice > Preach

1. Sebastian Junger, *Tribe: On Homecoming and Belonging* (New York: Twelve Books, 2016), 55.

2. Though this quote is consistently attributed to Father Gutiérrez, it appears to be more of a summation than a direct quotation. See Daniel Hartnett, "Remembering the Poor: An Interview with Gustavo Gutierrez," *America*, February 3, 2003, https://www.americamagazine.org/faith/2003/02/03/remembering-poor-interview-gustavo-gutierrez.

3. Gustavo Gutiérrez, *A Theology of Liberation: History, Politics, and Salvation*, rev. ed. (Maryknoll, NY: Orbis Books, 1988), xxxi.

4. For more information, visit the Asset-Based Community Development Institute at https://resources.depaul.edu/abcd-institute/Pages/default.aspx.

5. Courtney E. Martin, *Learning in Public: Lessons for a Racially Divided America from My Daughter's School* (New York: Little, Brown, 2021).

6. Gregory Boyle, *Tattoos on the Heart: The Power of Boundless Compassion* (New York: Free Press, 2011), 67.

7. Sister Helen Prejean (@helenprejean), "Being kind in an unjust system," Twitter, September 3, 2017, https://twitter.com/helenprejean/status/904366113521364994.

8. Kathy Park Hong, *Minor Feelings: An Asian American Reckoning* (New York: One World, 2020), 109.

9. Martin Luther King Jr., "Letter from Birmingham Jail: April 16, 1963," Grace Presbytery, accessed January 28, 2022, https://www.gracepresbytery

.org/wp-content/uploads/2020/06/Letter-from-a-Birmingham-Jail-King
.pdf.

10. Erin Moon, "Lil Treasures #69: Birthdays and Getting Out of Slumps," *The Swipe Up*, March 26, 2021, https://erinhmoon.substack
.com/p/lil-treasures-69?utm_source=url.

Chapter 9 Roots > Wheels

1. @kalalu, "We don't have the luxury," comment on Shannan Martin (@shannanwrites), Instagram, August 7, 2021, https://www.instagram
.com/p/CSTCYsug2se/.

2. Tiffany Shlain, *24/6: The Power of Unplugging One Day a Week* (New York: Gallery Books, 2019).

3. Helen Keller, *Let Us Have Faith* (repr., Garden City, NY: Doubleday & Co., 1946), 51.

4. "Trees in the Urban Environment: 'Seeing' Roots Underground," Open Access News, November 14, 2018, https://www.openaccessgovernment
.org/trees-urban-environment-roots-underground/54473/.

5. Leonard Cohen, "Anthem," *The Future* (New York: Legacy, 1992).

6. Shannan Martin (@shannanwrites), "Yesterday someone asked me an excellent question about neighbors," Instagram, August 7, 2021, https://www.instagram.com/p/CSTCYsug2se/.

7. @phdnofuddy, "Today one of my neighbors," comment on Shannan Martin (@shannanwrites), Instagram, August 7, 2021.

8. @jan_dm, "My parents met friends," comment on Shannan Martin (@shannanwrites).

9. @betsymcgill, "There's something comforting about knowing," comment on Shannan Martin (@shannanwrites).

10. @fidmomma, "Years ago, a new neighbor moved in," comment on Shannan Martin (@shannanwrites).

11. @chermcb, "Just last night our neighbor," comment on Shannan Martin (@shannanwrites).

12. @phookstra, "A new baby was born," comment on Shannan Martin (@shannanwrites).

13. Robin Wall Kimmerer, *Braiding Sweetgrass: Indigenous Wisdom, Scientific Knowledge and the Teachings of Plants* (Minneapolis: Milkweed Editions, 2015), 15.

Chapter 10 Empathy > Everything

1. Theresa Wiseman, "A Concept Analysis of Empathy," *Journal of Advanced Nursing* 23, no. 6 (June 1996): 1162–67.

2. Latasha Morrison, "Be the Bridge 230: Jamie Ivey," *Be the Bridge*

(podcast), August 10, 2021, https://anchor.fm/be-the-bridge/episodes/Be-The-Bridge-230---Jamie-Ivey-e151p6i.

3. "Brené Brown on Empathy," YouTube video, 2:53, uploaded by RSA, December 10, 2013, https://youtu.be/1Evwgu369Jw.

4. Danté Stewart (@stewartdantec), "Loving people is not simply asking," Instagram, September 10, 2021, https://www.instagram.com/p/CTpLA7NrmX3/.

5. Courtney E. Martin, *Learning in Public*, 325.

6. Green, *Anthropocene Reviewed*, 357.

7. Diana Oestreich, *Waging Peace: One Soldier's Story of Putting Love First* (Minneapolis: Broadleaf Books, 2020), 153.

8. Julie Hale, "Jennifer Longo: The Foster Care Novel That Was Waiting to Be Told," *Book Page*, January 23, 2020, https://www.bookpage.com/interviews/24820-jennifer-longo-ya/.

Shannan Martin is the author of *Falling Free*, *The Ministry of Ordinary Places*, and *Start with Hello*. She is a speaker and writer who found her voice in the country and her story in the city. She and her jail-chaplain husband, Cory, have four funny children and enjoy neighborhood life in Goshen, Indiana, a place they fall more in love with every year.

Connect with
SHANNAN MARTIN

To learn more about Shannan, neighboring, and soup, follow her online!

ShannanMartin.com